ASWB
Clinical Exam
Practice Questions

DEAR FUTURE EXAM SUCCESS STORY

First of all, **THANK YOU** for purchasing Mometrix study materials!

Second, congratulations! You are one of the few determined test-takers who are committed to doing whatever it takes to excel on your exam. **You have come to the right place.** We developed these practice tests with one goal in mind: to deliver you the best possible approximation of the questions you will see on test day.

Standardized testing is one of the biggest obstacles on your road to success, which only increases the importance of doing well in the high-pressure, high-stakes environment of test day. Your results on this test could have a significant impact on your future, and these practice tests will give you the repetitions you need to build your familiarity and confidence with the test content and format to help you achieve your full potential on test day.

Your success is our success

We would love to hear from you! If you would like to share the story of your exam success or if you have any questions or comments in regard to our products, please contact us at **800-673-8175** or **support@mometrix.com**.

Thanks again for your business and we wish you continued success!

Sincerely,
The Mometrix Test Preparation Team

TABLE OF CONTENTS

Practice Test #1

1. A child referral is underweight and shows evidence of poor hygiene. The most likely cause is:

    a. child abuse.
    b. child neglect.
    c. emotional neglect.
    d. failure to thrive.

2. Jenny is apathetic and irresponsible in her parenting. Audrey feels isolated, depressed and rejected by her own parents. Which of these women is more likely to be abusive to her child?

    a. Audrey
    b. Jenny
    c. They are equally likely
    d. Neither

3. Abusive parents are more likely to:

    a. have children close together in age.
    b. experience marital problems.
    c. fight physically.
    d. all of the above.

4. Using dolls with children who have been sexually abused can help primarily in what way?

    a. Relaxing children
    b. Helping children to understand body parts
    c. Encouraging control over the children's own bodies
    d. None of the above

5. What are three systems that contribute to the well-being of individuals?

    a. Formal, informal and organizational
    b. Natural, informal and societal
    c. Formal, informal and societal
    d. Normative, societal and formal

6. One of the two key ecological concepts in ecological systems theory is:

    a. the cultural aspects of the environment.
    b. level of fit.
    c. the system of enterprise.
    d. ecological reciprocity.

7. A drug-addicted individual's expectation of how a drug will make him feel:

    a. has a significant effect upon how the drug's effects are experienced.
    b. diminishes a drug's effects.
    c. does not impact the actual effects of the drug.
    d. can negate a drug's actual effect.

8. In Erikson's eight-stage model of psychosocial development, which stage could be negatively affected by inappropriate toilet training, leading to an "anal-retentive" or "anal-expressive" personality type later in life?

    a. Trust versus mistrust
    b. Autonomy versus shame
    c. Initiation versus guilt
    d. Industry versus inferiority

9. According to Sigmund Freud's psychoanalytic view, human behavior is influenced by what?

    a. The conscious mind
    b. The subconscious mind
    c. Repressed anxiety
    d. Recessive traits

10. Considering Sigmund Freud's theory regarding the effect of the subconscious upon behavior, what is one way an individual can control the influence of the subconscious?

    a. Remembering the past
    b. Repressing unconscious impulses
    c. By thinking before acting
    d. Eliminating unconscious drives

11. Who theorized the concept of an "ideal self"?

    a. Sigmund Freud
    b. Jean Piaget
    c. Alfred Adler
    d. Erik Erikson

12. Which chemical is known as the one that accompanies bonding behavior between mothers and children and between lovers?

    a. Serotonin
    b. Dopamine
    c. Oxytocin
    d. Oxycontin

13. Fredrick and Laura Perls are known for which of the following theories?

    a. Person-centered
    b. Gestalt
    c. Adlerian
    d. Psychoanalytic

14. Existentialism emphasizes:

    a. change.
    b. the past.
    c. the present.
    d. the unconscious.

15. A family therapist asks the daughter to place other members of her family in positions that she feels demonstrates their current relationships to each other. The daughter places the mother and son very close together, with the teenage son's hand leaning on his mother's shoulder. She places her father at the door, with his hand on the doorknob, but facing his wife. Finally, she puts herself in a chair at the far end of the room, as if she is observing the others, but not part of the group. In this sculpting technique, what is the client MOST likely saying about her family?

    a. She is demonstrating a family secret
    b. She is showing enmeshment between mother and son
    c. She is showing this family's low cohesion
    d. She is showing her lack of attachment

16. Operant conditioning is associated with what?

    a. Psychoanalytic theory
    b. Gestalt theory
    c. Behavioral theory
    d. Existential theory

17. Who performed experiments with salivating dogs to demonstrate classical conditioning?

    a. B. F. Skinner
    b. Ivan Pavlov
    c. Albert Bandura
    d. Albert Ellis

18. The family functioning scale was developed by which of the following?

    a. Carl Rogers
    b. Ludwig Geismer
    c. Jean Piaget
    d. B. F. Skinner

19. Which of the following has the most powerful effect upon an individual's response to stress?

    a. Gender
    b. IQ
    c. Social support
    d. Age

20. The primary risk factor for post-traumatic stress disorder (PTSD) is:

    a. IQ.
    b. gender.
    c. age.
    d. severity of exposure.

21. A client named Beverly has a well-paying job and lovely home; however, she has no family and is rather isolated from others. Another client, John, is unemployed and divorced but has an extensive social life. Both clients experience a significant crisis in their lives. Who is more likely to require intervention as a result?
    a. Beverly
    b. John
    c. Neither is likely to require intervention
    d. Both are equally likely to require intervention

22. Jean is recovering from the loss of her 95-year-old grandmother who died in her sleep. Bob was recently the victim of a violent crime. Who is more likely to require crisis intervention as a result of the recent stressful experience?
    a. Jean
    b. Bob
    c. Neither is likely to require intervention
    d. Both are equally likely to require intervention

23. The "acute" stage of the crisis state is thought to last:
    a. six to eight weeks.
    b. a variable length, depending on several factors.
    c. one to three weeks.
    d. one to seven days.

24. The crisis state is:
    a. pathological.
    b. abnormal.
    c. maladaptive.
    d. non-pathological.

25. Which theorist researched children's cognitive development and referred to the "preoperational stage"?
    a. B. F. Skinner
    b. Sigmund Freud
    c. Jean Piaget
    d. John Watson

26. Harry's mother is extremely concerned that her son is not crawling at 7 months of age, because "all the other children in his playgroup are." She wants to have him evaluated for a disability, despite the fact that in every other way, his development is quite normal. What is the FIRST thing the caseworker should suggest?
    a. A medical evaluation
    b. Play therapy
    c. Waiting another 90 days to see what happens
    d. Therapy for his anxious mother

27. In childhood development, what is the difference between private and social speech?
   a. Private occurs among family members only, and social with everyone else
   b. Social speech involves communication with strangers, and private with friends
   c. Private is with oneself, and social with others
   d. There is no difference between the two

28. What type of development does the Stanford-Binet scale measure?
   a. Intellectual development
   b. Physical maturation
   c. Language acquisition
   d. Psycho-social development

29. What type of development do the Wechsler Scales measure?
   a. Intellectual development
   b. Physical maturation
   c. Language acquisition
   d. Psycho-social development

30. Simon is 66 years old and was recently ordered by the court to attend counseling for an outburst in a grocery store, where he threw a can of pop at the clerk for being too slow in ringing up his purchases. His wife attends the first session as well, and although he insists his memory is "as good as it ever was," she shakes her head. He seems distracted and angry; she placates him, but he lashes out verbally. When the caseworker asks her if anything has changed recently, she tells him that Simon has always been a good-natured, easygoing man, but that lately he has been "difficult." As they are leaving, Simon, looking puzzled, says, "I don't even know why we're here."
What is the FIRST possible diagnosis a caseworker would consider in this case?
   a. Alcoholism
   b. Alzheimer's disease
   c. Bipolar disorder
   d. Impulse-control disorder

31. Both Don and Patrick have jobs they dislike. Don has few options but to stay with his current employment; however, Patrick has other skills that could recommend him for another position. Which man is less likely to suffer the effects of stress because of his job?
   a. Don
   b. Both have the same level of risk
   c. Patrick
   d. Neither has any risk at all

32. Unlike Freud, Carl Jung believed that people:
   a. change throughout life.
   b. have personalities that are determined in childhood.
   c. are strongly motivated by sexuality.
   d. can find meaning in dream symbols.

5

33. A young man with autism shows swift improvement when he is paired with a horse and starts learning to ride. His parents remove him from the program, citing an inability to drive him to the stables, and they refuse to allow the social worker to provide alternative transportation. The man speedily reverts to his self-harming behaviors and has to be hospitalized. From a systems standpoint, what is the MOST likely explanation for his parents' decision?
   a. They simply could not provide the needed transportation
   b. Systems cannot tolerate change
   c. The parents were protecting their son from outside influences
   d. The parents were unconsciously reestablishing the homeostasis of their system

34. Jane's husband expects her to create fabulous dinner parties for his boss, to be the perfectly available mother to their children, and to be ready for sex several nights a week. He also expects her to continue working the 12-hour shifts of a registered nurse. What problem is Jane MOST likely experiencing?
   a. Role complementarity
   b. Role discomplementarity
   c. Role ambiguity
   d. Role overload

35. Janet's husband recently died in a car accident. Her behavior of crying and choice of isolation most accurately refer to her being:
   a. bereaved.
   b. in a state of mourning.
   c. upset.
   d. sad.

36. Which of the following is one of Elisabeth Kübler-Ross's five stages of dying?
   a. Emotional upheaval
   b. Futility
   c. Fear
   d. Denial

37. What does the "hurried child" refer to?
   a. Adults who cling to their childhoods
   b. Children who are pressured to grow up too quickly
   c. A child with pronounced physical maturation
   d. Children who are slow to develop emotionally

38. A common point in defining culture is that it is:
   a. learned through socialization.
   b. inherited from family to family.
   c. stereotypic.
   d. none of the above.

39. Rose often becomes frustrated in school, makes loud noises in public, and doesn't understand what people are saying to her. She often seems rude. To her trusted teacher, she fluently describes a life of loneliness and confusion, but even in her family, no one understands her. She cannot read as well as most adolescents in her age group, but her IQ is quite high. However, she is considering not going to college because she thinks it would be too difficult. What is MOST likely Rose's problem?

   a. Rose has elective mutism
   b. Rose has autism
   c. Rose is hearing impaired
   d. Rose is visually impaired

40. What is the benefit of a "cultural match"?

   a. Enhanced insight into the client's situation
   b. Higher level of skill within the helper's culture
   c. Additional overall counseling skill
   d. There is no benefit

41. Stereotyping is often:

   a. a reasonable means of characterizing clients.
   b. a conscious attempt to define individuals.
   c. incorrect when addressing an entire group of people.
   d. useful in working with clients.

42. A social worker has her first counseling session with a young Native American man, and she finds it nearly impossible to get him to look her in the eye, much less to talk at any level beyond answering intake questions about his age and address. She is worried that he may be schizoid, although the school counselor who referred him gave a preliminary diagnosis of an adjustment disorder. What accounts for the difference in the counselors' opinions of the young man's problem?

   a. Inappropriate affect
   b. Cultural confusion
   c. Cultural competence
   d. Discrimination

43. In working with minority groups, what does "situational control" refer to?

   a. Maintaining order during the counseling session
   b. Placing restrictions on the client's home setting
   c. Factors that influence the client's life
   d. Factors that specifically influence the client's spirituality

44. What does "acculturation" refer to?

   a. The study of a particular culture
   b. Redefining cultural norms
   c. A subordinate culture emulating the dominant one
   d. The dominant culture emulating a subordinate one

45. When working with clients, professionals should keep in mind the words "known facts" as a means to help combat:
   a. inarticulation.
   b. avoidance issues.
   c. labeling.
   d. stereotypes.

46. In counseling situations, understanding behavioral cues can be:
   a. useful, but only in specific circumstances.
   b. minimally helpful.
   c. necessary because of cultural diversity.
   d. a means by which to lengthen the counseling session.

47. A recently retired middle-aged couple find themselves sharing their downsized home with their daughter, son-in-law, and two grandchildren. Although the situation is temporary, no one can predict when the younger couple will find work after losing their business to bankruptcy. The older couple find themselves stressed, and the time they had looked forward to spending in a second honeymoon is being spent with crying children and an overfilled house. They come to counseling to address their recently started, constant bickering. What is the FIRST thing their social worker should do?
   a. Bring in the younger couple for family counseling
   b. Provide job assistance to the younger couple
   c. Help the older couple find ways to support each other and their marriage
   d. Analyze the bickering and suggest alternative ways to communicate

48. A client presents with his wife who is complaining that the patient has had a change in cognitive function including language and memory. The client denies loss of pleasure in normal activities and denies feeling sad. The client is able to manage his medications but requires someone to set up his medication box and set a timer for him. The worker suspects:
   a. neurocognitive disorder.
   b. delirium.
   c. depression.
   d. schizophrenia.

49. A neurocognitive disorder could be specified as being due to which of the following?
   a. Vascular disease
   b. HIV infection
   c. Traumatic brain injury
   d. All of the above

50. For Autism spectrum disorders, which of the following should be specified?
   a. with rapid cycling
   b. with or without accompanying intellectual impairment
   c. if acute, subacute, or persistent
   d. with mood-congruent psychotic features

51. **What is the source of the DSM-5?**
    a. National Psychological Association
    b. National Counseling Group, Inc.
    c. National Association of Social Workers
    d. American Psychiatric Association

52. **An unmarried middle-aged client of Italian descent presents at a feminist therapy center with generalized anxiety and strongly conflicted feelings about her father. While she admits he "may be a little pushy," the examples she gives of her father's behavior toward her strike her counselor as being frankly domineering, sexist, and on the edge of abusive. But the client loves her father, describes him also as kind and protective of her, and is shocked when the counselor suggests that (for example) the father's recent attempt to "marry off" his daughter to a much older man is manipulative and highly inappropriate in modern-day American society. Which term MOST closely explains the behavior of the client's father?**
    a. Cultural bias
    b. Discrimination
    c. Cultural lag
    d. Culture-bound syndrome

53. **Evidence-based practice and measurement integrates knowledge gained from research with:**
    a. consumer values.
    b. clinical expertise.
    c. consumer surveys.
    d. both consumer values and clinical expertise.

54. **Social workers tend to primarily classify individuals in which of the following ways?**
    a. Abnormal vs. Normal
    b. Person-in-environment
    c. Disordered
    d. Interpersonal complexity

55. **In thinking specifically of person-in-environment (PIE), which is most likely to create social functioning difficulties?**
    a. Environmental unresponsiveness
    b. Medical disability
    c. A diagnosis of schizophrenia
    d. Panic disorder

56. **Interviewing requires a combination of which two types of skills?**
    a. Verbal and behavioral
    b. Behavioral and psychoanalytic
    c. Clinical and societal
    d. Learned and innate

57. In the initial interview, it often is best to ask as few direct questions as necessary for what reason?

    a. To modulate the course of treatment
    b. To allay any feelings of vulnerability in the client
    c. To lengthen the overall course of treatment
    d. None of the above

58. A family therapist tells her clients that one of the rules in her sessions is that "everybody talks." She asks each person to tell her what they think the main problem is, and she notices and sometimes even comments on nonverbal communications between family members that facilitate or hinder communication. What does this method do directly for the therapist, but only indirectly for the family?

    a. Formulates the problem using different perspectives
    b. Involves all members and gives each permission to speak
    c. Identifies family rules about who speaks and who typically gives or denies permission
    d. Delineates the power structure, hierarchies, and alliances in the family

59. The typical time period of onset for a substance abuse disorder is during what ages?

    a. Mid- to late adulthood
    b. Late adulthood
    c. Late adolescence to early adulthood
    d. None of the above

60. There is a high co-morbidity rate between substance abuse and:

    a. other disorders.
    b. yearly income.
    c. IQ.
    d. none of the above.

61. The core features of borderline personality disorder are often disagreed upon. However, two factors are common to the disorder—highly variable mood and:

    a. delusions.
    b. impulsive behavior.
    c. hallucinations.
    d. psychotic ideology.

62. Which does not describe a motivational obstacle arising from within the client?

    a. Abulia
    b. Amotivational syndrome
    c. Motivation-capacity-opportunity theory
    d. Apathy

63. In adults, manic episodes last for how long?

    a. A few hours
    b. At least 2 days
    c. At least one week
    d. At least 3 months

64. A manic episode first experienced after the age of 40 is:

    a. common.
    b. highly unusual.
    c. unlikely to be due to substance abuse.
    d. unlikely to be due to a medical condition.

65. Bipolar disorder easily can be confused with which of the following disorders?

    a. Borderline personality disorder
    b. Clinical depression
    c. Anxiety disorder
    d. Conduct disorder

66. Categories of risk for early-onset intellectual disability include which of the following?

    a. Problems at birth
    b. Poverty
    c. Age of verbal acquisition
    d. Both problems at birth and poverty

67. _____ is a disorder of thought, unlike _____ which is a disorder of mood.

    a. Borderline; conduct disorder
    b. Conduct disorder; depression
    c. Bipolar disorder; schizophrenia
    d. Schizophrenia; bipolar disorder

68. Jane has helped her client pinpoint his biggest problem and create a list of possible ways to address it. However, the client seems to find a problem with every intervention. When Jane suggests a relevant book, the client states that he doesn't read much. He refuses to join a group, saying he doesn't want to "meet a bunch of losers." He shoots down every possible intervention, and he even claims that, although it was his presenting problem and still causes him a great deal of suffering, there are other things he'd prefer to talk about in their sessions. What does this tell Jane about her work with this client?

    a. She has not found the right intervention and needs to try harder
    b. The client isn't motivated to change at this time
    c. She should refer this client to someone else
    d. The presenting problem wasn't the "real" problem: Jane should start over

69. Thought insertion/withdrawal refers to what?

    a. A psychoanalytic therapy technique
    b. The belief that thoughts are being put into or taken out of one's head
    c. A behavior therapy technique related to operant conditioning
    d. A type of hallucination

70. A disease characterized by a diffuse atrophy of the brain is:

    a. bipolar disorder.
    b. Alzheimer's.
    c. schizoaffective disorder.
    d. obsessive compulsive disorder.

71. Which type of sexual disorder is most likely to come to the attention of a social worker?
    a. Gender identity disorder
    b. Voyeurism
    c. Paraphilia
    d. Sexual function disorders

72. Frotteuristic disorder refers to a:
    a. personality disorder.
    b. symptom of schizophrenia.
    c. sexual disorder.
    d. common bipolar symptom.

73. Which of the following has criteria for diagnosis that it occurs for at least two years, more days than not, making it not very episodic?
    a. Bipolar disorder
    b. Disruptive mood dysregulation disorder
    c. Major depressive disorder
    d. Dysthymic disorder

74. Which is the most common lifetime disorder?
    a. Conduct disorder
    b. Depression
    c. Borderline personality disorder
    d. Schizophrenia

75. Which of the following can increase one's risk of attempting suicide in the future?
    a. Prior suicide ideation
    b. Past suicidal behavior in one's family
    c. History of frequent mobility
    d. All of the above

76. In psychoanalytic theory, four forces motivate behavior. Which of the following is one of them?
    a. Id
    b. Pleasure principle
    c. Subconscious
    d. Ego

77. Richard is in a highly agitated state. He repeatedly makes statements such as "I don't know why I can't just have what I want!" and "I should be able to do as I please." What Freudian part of the subconscious is Richard's behavior demonstrating?
    a. Pleasure principle
    b. Unconscious
    c. Id
    d. Defense mechanisms

78. In psychoanalytic therapy, there are three basic types of anxiety. An anti-abortion client is suffering emotional misgivings from an abortion she had a month ago. Which of the below types of anxiety would likely fit her situation?

 a. Reality anxiety
 b. Moral anxiety
 c. Neurotic anxiety
 d. None of the above

79. A client is suffering from a recent divorce and sense of abandonment. However, she presents multiple reasons why the divorce was a good thing and insists it was something she actually welcomed. Which of the following might explain her thoughts?

 a. Anxiety
 b. Anal stage regression
 c. Overactive superego
 d. Rationalization

80. At what level of care would a social worker investigate persons at risk of abuse or neglect, address the situation, prevent further risk, and locate resources or better placements for that person?

 a. Extended
 b. Skilled
 c. Intermediate
 d. Protective

81. Freud's final stage of personality development is:

 a. the genital stage.
 b. the latent stage.
 c. the oral stage.
 d. the phallic stage.

82. A social worker who prefers a psychoanalytic approach to counseling is working with Patricia, a teen diagnosed with a conduct disorder. In focusing on memories of past abuse, how is the social worker attempting to alter Patricia's problem behavior?

 a. Through "reeducating"
 b. Via "guided discovery"
 c. By listening to the client's thoughts
 d. By bringing the subconscious into consciousness

83. One way to modify a client's behavior (through the use of psychoanalytic therapy) is:

 a. to strengthen the ego.
 b. by "re-educating."
 c. through reciprocal determinism.
 d. through existentialism.

84. The psychoanalytic technique in which the social worker says a word and the client must say what immediately comes to mind is called:
a. interpretation.
b. free association.
c. discussion.
d. associative response.

85. Gestalt therapy seeks to understand the phenomenological aspects of the client. What does this refer to?
a. Memories
b. Perceptions
c. Dreams
d. Subconscious

86. How do gestalt social workers regard a client's past?
a. It is of no importance
b. It is significant
c. The present is more important
d. Significant, while the present is more important

87. In which of the following types of therapy does the social worker help the client clarify goals and move toward an "ideal self"?
a. Gestalt
b. Cognitive behavioral therapy
c. Adlerian
d. Freudian psychoanalysis

88. Albert Ellis, who espoused rational emotive behavior therapy (REBT), believed that abnormal behavior is a result of:
a. irrational thinking.
b. chemical imbalances in the brain.
c. subconscious drives.
d. rational thought processes.

89. "I just don't know what to do," a client says during a therapy session. "Sounds like you're feeling unsure of yourself right now," responds the social worker, while demonstrating a warm and respectful demeanor. The client continues by saying, "I hate women." The social worker asks, "You hate all women?" What is this style of therapy called?
a. Psychoanalytic
b. Rational emotive behavior therapy
c. Adlerian
d. Person-centered

90. The remedial model of group therapy focuses on _____, but the reciprocal model emphasizes _____.
a. individual change; the individual and society
b. the individual and society; individual change
c. social goals; the individual and society
d. family structure; individual change

91. When selecting members for group therapy, does the age of individual members make a difference?
  a. Never
  b. Only if specified by the agency
  c. Sometimes
  d. Always

92. The description of "open" or "closed" in regard to therapy groups refers to what?
  a. Timing of admission
  b. Type of group members
  c. Gender of group members
  d. Length of group sessions

93. Family therapy sessions reveal a client who reacts emotionally (rather than rationally) to daily situations within the family. According to Bowen's family systems theory, the client may be described as:
  a. illogical.
  b. undifferentiated.
  c. differentiated.
  d. emotional.

94. In a family experiencing a great deal of conflict, especially between spouses, the mother is expending significant time and effort upon her oldest, male child. How might this be explained in terms of Bowen's family systems theory?
  a. Differentiation of self
  b. Triangles
  c. Family project process
  d. Family projection process

95. A treatment goal of "improving the marital relationship" would be better stated in which way?
  a. Stating, "The client will spend one hour per day in one-to-one discussion with spouse"
  b. Several smaller, specific goals to achieve the greater goal
  c. Goals that are realistic and measurable
  d. All of the above

96. Listening to John discuss his upcoming marriage, his social worker responds, "Sounds like you're feeling anxious." After mirroring back his comments for a few minutes, the social worker then explores the possibility that if John would think differently about his marriage, he might come to feel differently. Later in the session, the social worker guides an exercise in which she states a word and John immediately responds with the first word that pops into his head. Which of the following best explains what the social worker is doing?
  a. Selective eclecticism
  b. Selecting a professional psychosocial theory
  c. Emulating a specific theorist
  d. Inventing her own treatment method

97. Which of the following is one of the four main divisions in the casework process?

    a. Interpersonal intervention

    b. Ending

    c. Therapy choices

    d. Assessment

98. Sharon and Jack are forming a college therapy group, and they realize that the first five people to sign up have all been fairly extroverted women. They decide to place posters advertising the group in the computer labs of the chemistry, engineering, and mathematics departments. What are the coleaders trying to achieve?

    a. A structured group

    b. Group balance

    c. Group cohesiveness

    d. Group harmony

99. Modeling in therapy refers to:

    a. an artistic endeavor.

    b. imitation.

    c. a therapy technique specifically designed to enhance group communication.

    d. a technique developed for use with clients diagnosed with Asperger syndrome.

100. A social worker has been facilitating a therapy group of chronic overeaters for three months. During the most recent session, he observes several members defending the actions of other group members. He also observes a member who was thinking of leaving the group being universally urged to stay by the other members. Which of the following best describes this type of group behavior?

    a. Minimizing distractions

    b. Moving apart

    c. Getting along

    d. Sticking together

101. In an initial group session, each member is instructed to share a positive (yet not too personal) memory with the group. What is the likely purpose of this activity?

    a. To keep group members' expectations clear

    b. To make members comfortable in the group setting

    c. To set the standard for future sessions

    d. To encourage members to guard their thoughts and feelings

102. All aspects of the helping relationship depend upon:

    a. body language.

    b. verbal language.

    c. communication.

    d. therapeutic skill.

103. Mark is 40 years old. He has been diagnosed with posttraumatic stress disorder (PTSD) and attention-deficit/hyperactivity disorder (ADHD). He has had several relationships with women that included violence. He comes to the agency as an involuntary client after receiving a ticket for texting while driving and having been fired from his job for watching online pornography. He admits to spending hours each day on porn sites, spending hundreds of dollars each month on them. Which would be the BEST hypothesis about Mark's youth?

   a. He had a learning disorder
   b. He had ADHD
   c. He was sexually abused
   d. He was addicted to drugs or alcohol

104. A type of communication often overlooked as a therapeutic tool is:

   a. silence.
   b. body language.
   c. verbal cues.
   d. anger.

105. Twenty-three-year-old Robert is seeing a social worker because of abuse he suffered during his early childhood. Every time the discussion turns toward a particular memory of an abusive interaction, omissions are obvious in the material he relates. Some of the verbalized information also seems to ill-fit the situation he is recalling. What might this behavior be due to?

   a. Confusion
   b. Illogical thinking
   c. Resistance
   d. Either illogical thinking or resistance

106. Janet has been seeing a social worker for several weeks. Ten minutes into a session, the tone of her voice alters obviously. To what might this be attributed?

   a. Fatigue
   b. Boredom
   c. Emotional attachment
   d. None of the above

107. It's significant to learn if a client takes responsibility for self or others because:

   a. it's reflective of one's responsibility to resolve issues.
   b. a martyr personality is more resistant to therapy.
   c. self-responsibility is counter-productive.
   d. all of the above.

108. Being empathetic to the client in a therapeutic relationship refers to which of the following?

   a. Feeling what the client is feeling
   b. Condoning what the client is feeling
   c. Identifying with the client's feelings
   d. Understanding the client's feelings

109. Kelly spends a lot of time and energy dealing with her husband's drinking problem. She hides his liquor or pours it down the drain, and then she feels sorry for him and goes to the store to buy more. When he goes "cold turkey," his suffering is so extreme that she gives him a drink "just to get him over the hump." He blames her for making him want to drink, and she accepts that if she were easier to get along with, he would be able to maintain his sobriety. What is the clinical term for Kelly's attempts to help her husband, which also helps him keep drinking?

    a. Codependency
    b. Enabling
    c. Passive aggression
    d. Misplaced empathy

110. Which quality specifically aids a social worker in avoiding the inclination to say things only to please a client?

    a. Self-confidence
    b. Intellect
    c. Sense of humor
    d. Excellent documentation skills

111. Janice has been seeing a social worker for marital difficulties. A few weeks into counseling, she relates memories of a childhood conflict with her brother that she reports was painful for her. However, in her description of events, the experience does not sound particularly significant. Which of the following possibilities should the social worker be alert to?

    a. The client is lying
    b. The events discussed have been altered to seem more socially acceptable
    c. The client's memory of events is inaccurate
    d. All of the above

112. A social worker's initial interview with John runs smoothly. They discuss his feelings of anxiety about his new job, and he verbalizes concrete plans to manage it. The social worker demonstrates a supportive, respectful demeanor in a warm setting. What is the most likely reason that John never returns for treatment?

    a. He didn't like how he was treated
    b. His needs were met through the initial interaction with him
    c. He is "resistant"
    d. The social worker's skills are lacking

113. A social worker asks her client multiple follow-up questions in response to what he is describing, even though she thinks she understands what he's saying. What is the social worker demonstrating?

    a. Positive facilitation skills
    b. Good interviewing skills
    c. Being a good listener
    d. An attentive nature

114. Jamie is being counseled to aid in dealing with her fear of intimacy. During a session, the social worker notes that whenever her mother's name is mentioned, Jamie's responses become shorter and she quickly changes the subject. What should the social worker do?

a. Increase Jamie's comfort level by avoiding the subject of her mother
b. Focus attention on the issue of Jamie's mother
c. Ignore the mother issue, as it's not significant
d. Use the mother issue to springboard into gaining more information about other family members

115. Which disorder MOST frequently occurs in association with addictive disorders, with approximately 30% of people with addictions also experiencing this problem?

a. Bipolar disorder
b. Anxiety
c. Depression
d. Obsessive-compulsive disorder (OCD)

116. Janet twists her fingers together in her lap as she says she is no longer concerned about her upcoming surgery. She further states (with a slight change in the tone of her voice) that she has come to terms with her diagnosis of breast cancer. If a social worker is listening to his client with his "third ear" in this instance, what is he doing?

a. Listening for hidden meaning
b. Interpreting behavioral cues
c. Observing verbal inflection in tone
d. All of the above

117. Social workers sometimes make the "mistake of assumption," especially in the initial counseling session. What does this refer to?

a. Accepting the presenting problem as the actual or only problem
b. Listening ineffectively
c. Not focusing on the presenting problem
d. Focusing on the level of vocalization

118. A social worker should always be available to the client, within reasonable limits. However, because availability is a "double-edged sword," a social worker must:

a. allow for issues of vacation time and work schedules.
b. maintain a set schedule.
c. ensure availability at all times.
d. set strict boundaries on availability.

119. An elderly client tearfully states, "My children lead very busy lives. It seems like every moment of their time is scheduled with one thing or another." What is a likely underlying, unstated feeling within this comment?

a. Perplexed
b. Inadequate
c. Unappreciated
d. All of the above

120. A client verbalizes discontent regarding the progress of his treatment plan. The social worker asks, "Are you saying you're not pleased with your progress up to this point?" The social worker then adds, "You sound upset" and reassures the client that "things will get better soon." This communication involves several errors. Which of the following is one of them?

- a. A lack of demonstrated warmth and empathy on the part of the social worker
- b. A response that isn't confrontational enough
- c. Inappropriate reassurance
- d. A focus on conscious thoughts

121. A client is seeing a social worker for difficulties he's experiencing with family conflicts and discusses his employment in the family business. He comments, "I like working that lousy job with my brother. When all is said and done, I really respect that idiot brother of mine." Which of the following does this comment bring to mind?

- a. Positive communication
- b. Freudian conflict
- c. Disqualifying communication
- d. Thought/feeling confusion

122. In a session of couple's counseling, the following exchange takes place:

Jan: "I would prefer it if you would stop calling me names when you're angry."
Bob: "You shouldn't make me angry if you don't want to be called names."

What is the relationship message of this communication between Jan and Bob?

- a. Jan doesn't like to be called names
- b. Jan feels negatively about being called names
- c. Bob is dominant in the relationship
- d. Bob doesn't take responsibility for his actions

123. _____ is often referred to as a circular reciprocally interacting process.

- a. Therapy
- b. Communication
- c. Operant conditioning
- d. The initial counseling interview

124. An 18-year-old client presents with an aloof manner that is indifferent and withdrawn. He has no friends and spends most of his time outside of school building model airplanes. He does not fit the criteria for autism disorders. His mother tells the social worker that he's always been "different; impossible to talk to; not a bad boy, just not really there, somehow." What is the most likely DSM-5 diagnosis for this young man?

- a. Schizoid disorder of adolescence
- b. Schizophreniform disorder
- c. Schizoid personality disorder
- d. Highly introverted personality

125. A social worker notices that when working with clients who have health complaints, he experiences emotional irritation and has little patience for encouraging such discussion. What should the social worker do?

    a. Nothing, as every social worker has points of irritation
    b. Self-examine to determine possible reasons for the reaction
    c. Take steps to ensure that he no longer treats clients of this type
    d. Report the difficulty immediately to his supervisor

126. A client's main goal is to be free of conflict when called upon to make a decision. She has suffered for years with being unable to make efficient choices and never again wants to experience anxiety when debating a choice. What is likely to happen in terms of counseling?

    a. The client will be happy during the course of counseling
    b. Counseling will be of a short-term nature
    c. She will effectively meet her therapy goal with time and patience
    d. Counseling will become interminable

127. A client has been in therapy for several months because of depression and suicide ideation. Progress has been limited until, during a particular session, the client demonstrates a positive attitude and reports he has "turned a corner" and finally feels relaxed and happy. What should his social worker do?

    a. Take a position of extreme caution
    b. Feel good that the client has finally "turned a corner"
    c. Make plans to terminate counseling because the client has improved
    d. Continue with counseling as usual

128. A client is the same gender as the social worker and not homosexual. The client is seeing the social worker because of relationship issues. During the course of treatment, it becomes apparent that the client is directing feelings of a romantic nature toward the social worker. What is likely to be the cause of the client's feelings?

    a. An unhealthy attachment to the social worker
    b. A genuine romantic attraction to the social worker
    c. Transference
    d. None of the above

129. Helping people and addressing social problems falls under which of the following NASW social worker values?

    a. Service
    b. Social justice
    c. Dignity
    d. Competence

130. Challenging social injustice addresses which of the following social work values?

    a. Service
    b. Social justice
    c. Dignity
    d. Competence

131. Personal worth is a value that aligns with which of the following NASW values?

a. Dignity
b. Social justice
c. Competence
d. Service

132. Strengthening the connection between two factors is a primary ethical principle of social workers. What does this relate to?

a. Integrity
b. Competence
c. Human relationships
d. Social justice

133. Which of the following is NOT considered a neurobiological disorder?

a. Anorexia nervosa
b. Schizophrenia
c. Bipolar disorder
d. Major depression

134. Clients have an ethical right to self-determination. When may a social worker limit this right?

a. When there's a threat to self or others
b. If the client is choosing poorly
c. When the courts are involved
d. If the client's family is opposed to a particular action

135. In the course of explaining her marital problems, a client also alludes to various symptoms that could be diagnosed as psychotic in nature. Her social worker doesn't have training in psychosis and should:

a. continue to work with the client but research psychosis.
b. consult with a social worker trained in psychosis.
c. discontinue counseling and refer the client to another social worker.
d. discontinue counseling because the social worker isn't qualified in this case.

136. A client reveals to his social worker that he has recently entered into a business relationship with the social worker's spouse. Is this likely to present a concern?

a. Yes, but only if the counseling relationship has just begun
b. Yes, but only if money is involved
c. Yes
d. No

137. A social worker has recently entered into a counseling relationship with a client who has a past history of depression and suicide attempts. The social worker will want to give particular care to discussing:

a. the limits of confidentiality.
b. the legal definition of suicide.
c. his experience in treating patients who are depressed.
d. the effects of suicide upon family and friends.

138. A client wants to read his personal records. What should the social worker do?

 a. Deny the request and explain that records are private
 b. Provide the records and help to interpret them
 c. Allow the client to see only those parts that are pertinent
 d. Deny the request

139. An individual with whom a social worker has had a previous sexual relationship has arrived in her office seeking counseling for an addiction problem. What should the social worker do?

 a. Begin counseling, because the relationship is in the past
 b. Enter into a co-therapy situation
 c. Design a treatment plan but refer to a colleague
 d. Refer the client to another social worker

140. When engaging in physical contact with a client, what should be considered?

 a. The cultural significance of physical contact
 b. The possibility of psychological harm
 c. Clear boundaries for physical contact
 d. All of the above

141. A 70-year-old man is referred to a social worker for confusion, emotionality, and unusual lethargy. In the session, he mentions having headaches and needing help organizing his daily schedule of medications. What is the FIRST thing the social worker should do for this client before working with him in therapy?

 a. Have him assessed for Alzheimer's disease
 b. Assess his reality orientation
 c. Help him schedule an appointment for a review of his medications
 d. Ask if he is depressed

142. A social worker and client feel a physical attraction toward each other and mutually wish to enter into a personal relationship. What should the social worker do?

 a. Terminate both counseling and the relationship, and refer to a colleague
 b. Terminate counseling, refer to a colleague and pursue a relationship
 c. Continue counseling but ignore the attraction
 d. Continue counseling while addressing their feelings during the sessions

143. A social worker's colleague is clearly incompetent in working with marital issues but continues to offer services for those in marital conflict. What should the social worker's first step be?

 a. Document his concerns
 b. Contact the NASW
 c. Meet with his colleague about his concerns
 d. Meet with his own supervisor

144. A school shooting occurs at a nearby high school. Authorities are publicly requesting social workers to assist in working with students. Which of the following is true of a social worker's professional obligation?

    a. He is ethically expected to help if he can
    b. He is under no obligation to assist
    c. He should organize other social workers to help
    d. He needs to educate the public about the situation

145. The subjects recruited for a research project may alter their behavior if they know the possible risks. What should the researchers do?

    a. Keep the specifics of the project confidential
    b. Inform the subjects of the risks and obtain their consent
    c. Tell the subjects as little as possible to maintain the integrity of the research
    d. Hide the specifics of the research until after it's complete

146. A social worker is asked to supervise new social workers who recently have been hired by an organization. The social worker has extensive experience working with the client population these new hires will serve and therefore is viewed as the best person to oversee them. Which of the following best describes that social worker's new role?

    a. Authority model
    b. Team supervisor
    c. Competence model
    d. Organizational supervisor

147. A social worker and her colleagues meet regularly to discuss cases and progress. Each member of the group offers insight and suggestions within an atmosphere of mutual respect and sharing, and members are ultimately responsible for their own work. Which of the following refers to this type of supervision model?

    a. Peer supervision model
    b. Team supervision model
    c. Organizational supervision model
    d. None of the above

148. In an autonomous practice, a social worker is:

    a. given a direct one-to-one supervisor.
    b. not expected to have a supervisor.
    c. expected to meet regularly for peer review.
    d. all of the above.

149. A social worker supervising a new social worker in her agency monitors his workload and assesses his stress level. She reviews his adherence to agency policy and also compares his educational training to the population he is currently serving. Which of the following refers to the type of supervision she is providing?

    a. Administrative supervision
    b. Supervisory-function supervision
    c. Supportive supervision
    d. Educational supervision

150. It is often said that a critical component of the supervisory relationship is "shared meaning." To what does this refer?
   a. When both people "mean" to say the same thing
   b. When supervisor and supervisee share the same motivation
   c. Shared feelings between the supervisor and supervisee
   d. Mutual understanding and agreement

151. A social worker in a crisis center wants to research women who come there as victims of sexual assault. He hopes that his efforts will help provide insight into assault survivors everywhere. What type of generalization underlies his view of his research?
   a. Cross-population generalization
   b. Sample generalization
   c. Random generalization
   d. None of the above

152. A supervisor presents a social worker with research findings that include pages of graphs, statistical analysis and numerical listings. What type of research method does this likely represent?
   a. Correlational
   b. Randomized
   c. Qualitative
   d. Quantitative

153. A team of eight social workers provides services to area migrant workers. The team supervisor meets regularly with them to monitor performance, assign work, set goals and perform any other tasks necessary. In this team approach to service delivery, who has the final say regarding the decisions being made?
   a. The clients
   b. The CEO of the agency worked for
   c. Each member has equal authority
   d. The team supervisor

154. What is likely to be the most important psychological component of the supervisory relationship?
   a. Trust
   b. Honesty
   c. Focus
   d. Warmth

155. Service delivery standards often are set by policy that is created through:
   a. incremental process.
   b. a series of steps.
   c. cyclical patterns.
   d. all of the above.

156. Social workers who understand policy and recognize the barriers clients may face in receiving services tend to be effective at:
   a. maximizing clients' access to benefits.
   b. lowering the cost of services.
   c. de-stigmatizing client services.
   d. avoiding stereotypes.

157. Research indicates that when clients are involved in decision-making regarding services, they tend to be more pleased with the overall approach. However, some clients may not find this preferable. Which of the following might those be?
   a. Dementia clients
   b. Low IQ individuals
   c. Head injury clients
   d. All of the above

158. A facility provides services based on what its staff determines is needed. This type of service delivery is called:
   a. consumer case management.
   b. consumer-driven.
   c. provider-driven.
   d. client-controlled care.

159. Attempts to quantify and measure service delivery aid in:
   a. increasing the efficiency of services.
   b. predicting the cost of services.
   c. determining the effectiveness of services offered.
   d. all of the above.

160. One year after a new program for youth has been implemented at a facility, a social worker questions how the program is being run and how well it has met its goals. This type of evaluation addresses process and outcome, which enables staff to measure the three E's of:
   a. efficiency, effectiveness and efficacy.
   b. effort, efficiency and excellence.
   c. effort, efficiency and effectiveness.
   d. excellence, efficacy and evaluation.

161. The stages of grief as theorized by Elizabeth Kubler-Ross include denial, anger, bargaining, depression, and acceptance. What is an important fact that she discussed after publication of her work and that many practitioners are not aware of?
   a. The listed stages are not relevant to people undergoing any loss but bereavement
   b. The stages can only be passed through in the order listed above
   c. The stages are not necessarily passed through in order, and they may even be revisited
   d. The stages do not apply to people facing their own death

162. Because the facility where he works does not depend on client files and record-keeping for its funding, a social worker decides to keep only minimal notes on his client contacts. Is this a good idea?

    a. Yes
    b. No, never
    c. Maybe
    d. Only if his direct supervisor approves

163. A type of record-keeping that involves a detailed chronological order of treatment including a face sheet, contracts, client interpretations and in-depth contact information for everyone involved in treatment is called:

    a. process recording.
    b. problem-oriented recording.
    c. narrative records or ledgers.
    d. diagnostic recording.

164. Audio and video recording as a type of record-keeping is often used in what settings?

    a. Human services organizations
    b. Medical settings
    c. Educational settings
    d. Both medical settings and educational settings

165. SOAP refers to what type of record-keeping?

    a. Audio/visual recording
    b. Process recording
    c. Diagnostic recording
    d. Problem-oriented recording

166. Although a social worker feels comfortable with her level of practice and the record-keeping where she works, she is unsure about the overall success rate of the organization and her services. How might GAS help?

    a. It formulates the sustainability of treatment measures
    b. Through systematic review of client/ social worker interaction
    c. By providing specific measurement of treatment goals
    d. It allows for transportation of documents

167. A social worker often is required to work collaboratively with nurses. He notes that conflicts often arise in determining client needs and how best to provide treatment. What might be the most likely cause of such discord?

    a. The medical model
    b. Simple personality differences
    c. Long-standing medical animosity toward social workers
    d. Antiquated policies

168. As part of John's initial assessment, a social worker takes a medication history of the prescription as well as non-prescription medications John currently takes. Which of the following questions would best determine any other ways in which the client medicates himself?

    a.   Do you drink a lot of coffee?
    b.   Are you a big drinker?
    c.   Do you smoke a lot?
    d.   What do you do to relieve pain when you have a headache?

169. A treatment facility in a rural area on the outskirts of a city sees a high percentage of clients from the city on a weekly basis. A social worker proposes relocating to a building within the city limits. What would this be called?

    a.   A rational deduction
    b.   Community-based practice
    c.   City-service development
    d.   Community-oriented service

170. A social worker serves on a task force addressing the issue of child abuse. A former client of his who was seen because of abuse issues recently became a social worker and has been asked to serve on the same task force. What should the social worker do?

    a.   Make the group aware of the possible conflict but stay in the group
    b.   Stay on the task force because the client-social worker relationship is in the past
    c.   Resign from the task force immediately
    d.   It depends upon the particular complexities of the previous relationship

Answer Key and Explanations for Test #1

1. B: The most likely cause of the referral of a child that is underweight and shows evidence of poor hygiene is child neglect. Neglect is the answer because the child obviously is not receiving adequate care. Lack of proper nutrition and insufficient attention to hygiene suggest neglect rather than abuse.

2. A: Audrey is more likely to be abusive to her child. Abusive parents often have been abused as children themselves and feel rejected by their own parents. Neglectful parents tend more toward irresponsibility and often are ignorant of child developmental issues. Audrey's experiences with her parents and depression make her the more likely of the two women to be the abusive parent.

3. D: Parents who are abusive toward their children are more likely to engage in all of the listed options, in addition to experiencing more stressful events than most families and having a disorganized household. Abusive parents also tend to isolate themselves.

4. C: Doll therapy with children who have been sexually abused can help by encouraging control over the children's own bodies. Doll therapy has also been seen to help relax the child and help the child understand their body parts, but the encouragement of control over their own body is the primary benefit of this type of therapy.

5. C: Formal, informal and societal systems all contribute to the well-being of individuals. Informal systems are such things as family and the environment. Formal systems would be such things as community organizations, and an example of a societal system would be a government agency.

6. B: Ecological systems theory refers to the relationship and adaptation of organisms among themselves and within their environment. The level of fit between the person and the environment and the interaction between environments are the two key concepts in this systems theory.

7. A: Studies have shown that a drug-addicted individual's expectation of how a drug will make them feel has a significant effect upon how the drug's effects are experienced. For example, if the user expects to feel light-headed and euphoric, he likely will experience those sensations regardless of what sensations the drug is actually producing.

8. B: Autonomy versus shame takes place between the ages of 1 and 3, the time in life when children are being toilet trained. Erikson theorized that harsh toilet training methods would create withholding or "anal-retentive" personality traits, and that permissive toilet training would lead to "anal-expressive" traits.

9. B: According to Freud's psychoanalytic view, human behavior is influenced by the subconscious mind. Freud emphasized the role of the subconscious in people's lives and felt that it was connected to behavior. Freud believed that by bringing subconscious issues into conscious awareness, he could enhance understanding of an individual's behavior.

10. C: According to Freud, one way an individual can control the influence of the subconscious is by thinking before acting. Individuals may automatically react to situations based upon information stored in the subconscious. However, a client can be counseled to think before choosing a course of action and thus mitigate the effects of the subconscious upon behavior.

11. C: Alfred Adler theorized that individuals begin to form an idea of the "ideal self" around the age of six. The individual then works toward achieving that ideal self, choosing behavior that will aid in reaching the ideal

12. C: Oxytocin is known as the "love hormone." It is present during labor, breastfeeding, lovemaking, cuddling, and other bonding experiences such as playing with pets. As a drug, it has been used to precipitate labor.

13. B: Gestalt theory places an emphasis on present behavior and the awareness of what one is experiencing at any given moment. The client's view of what is being experienced, and the social worker's assistance in working through those feelings, can aid in altering behavior.

14. A: Existentialism theorizes that humans are in a constant state of change. People have ultimate control over their lives and behavior, even though they cannot always control their thoughts.

15. C: By removing the man from his wife and removing herself from the rest of the group, the daughter is showing that, although the mother and son have a close relationship, the family as a whole has split apart. This displays a sense of low cohesion.

16. C: Operant conditioning is associated with the work of B.F. Skinner, who theorized that an individual's behavior will be repeated if it is positively reinforced (behavioral therapy). On the other hand, behavior that is punished (or does not elicit a reaction) will be eliminated.

17. B: Ivan Pavlov is best known for his experiments with salivating dogs. He demonstrated classical conditioning, with the idea that if an unconditioned stimulus and response are paired often enough, the conditioned stimulus will produce an unconditioned response (behavior) on its own.

18. B: Ludwig Geismer's scale of family functioning was developed in the 1950s to assess the social functioning of families that were dysfunctional. It can be useful in assessment, treatment and/or research.

19. C: Research has shown that the degree of social support available to an individual can significantly affect how he or she reacts to life stressors and their possible negative outcomes. A firm social support structure can aid an individual in managing a stressful situation and bringing it to a successful, healthy resolution.

20. D: The primary risk factor for PTSD is the severity of exposure. Other factors to consider with PTSD are psychiatric symptoms, child abuse and previous multiple events, to name a few. While some risk factors are known, not as much is known about what affects the course of PTSD over time. However, a good social support system can be a positive factor in how a client deals with PTSD.

21. A: Beverly is more likely to require professional intervention (as a result of the crisis she has experienced) because she has little or no social support system. Studies have shown that people with good social support systems fare better in crises. John may have more "problems" in his life (which can make him more vulnerable to a crisis), but his social support system likely gives him the advantage over Beverly.

22. B: Bob is more likely to require crisis intervention as a result of the recent stressful experience. Natural crises in life (such as marriage, the birth of a child or the natural death of a loved one) are often less likely to produce severe distress than those crises that may be viewed as outside the expected human experience (such as violent crime and natural disasters). Therefore, in this case Bob is more likely to require intervention.

23. B: The acute stage of crisis is thought to last for a variable length, depending upon several factors. Although it previously was thought that the acute crisis state lasts between six and eight weeks, it's now believed that such a state can last much longer, depending upon the nature of the event, what it means to the individual, and the coping mechanisms at hand.

24. D: The crisis state is not, in and of itself, pathological in nature. Individuals can come through it, adapt and grow, becoming stronger for future crisis situations.

25. C: Jean Piaget researched children's cognitive development and referred to period between ages three and six as the "preoperational stage." In this state children can think in symbols even though they cannot yet use logic.

26. C: Although Harry's mother may think that his development is abnormally slow, most children start crawling between ages 7 and 10 months, and some even skip crawling and go straight to toddling. The mother seems to be comparing her son unfavorably (and maybe unrealistically) to the children in his playgroup, hoping to use his development to bolster the needs of her ego. The caseworker would do best to reassure the mother that Harry will crawl soon and to recommend patience with the natural process of his growth.

27. C: Private speech is with oneself, while social speech with others. Private speech (speaking aloud to oneself) is common in early and middle childhood, and ranges from repetitive words to thinking aloud. Social speech seeks to be understood by another person.

28. A: The Stanford-Binet Intelligence Scale was the first test of child intelligence to be developed. It evaluates levels of cognitive development rather than overall development.

29. A: The Wechsler Intelligence Scales measure intellectual development through IQ scores on both performance and verbal levels with a variety of subtests.

30. B: Simon's age, change of personality, aggressive behavior, and confusion point to senile dementia and possibly Alzheimer's disease.

31. C: Patrick is more likely to suffer the effects of stress because of his job. Research on animals and humans has shown a link between stressful situations that seem uncontrollable and illness. Patrick is likely to feel he has some control over his stress-producing situation, so he is less likely to suffer significant ill effects from it.

32. A: Unlike Sigmund Freud (who believed personality is set in childhood), Jung believed that people continue to grow and change throughout life. He believed that people suppress aspects of their personalities in order to meet responsibilities early in life, and later in life they bring those suppressed parts to the forefront.

33. D: Systems theory notes that even a positive change in one family member—especially that of the identified patient—disrupts the system, so that other family members attempt to get the family member to change back. Preventing change in one family member means the rest of the family can avoid change, even when it also means certain suffering.

34. D: Jane is attempting to fulfill the roles of wife, mother, breadwinner, and society hostess—some of the duties and time constraints of which must occasionally conflict. Although all of her assigned roles are traditionally "feminine" (even her arduous job is stereotypically "feminine") there are simply too many expectations to meet them all successfully—a condition of overload.

35. A: Bereavement is a state of being, specifically a change in status. Because Janet was a wife and is now a widow, bereavement speaks to that change. Mourning refers to behavior associated with Janet's bereavement (her crying and choice of isolation).

36. D: Kübler-Ross's five stages of dying are denial, anger, bargaining, depression and acceptance. People may experience the stages in differing orders, and some people may skip one or more stages altogether.

37. B: The "hurried child" refers to children that are pressured to grow up too quickly. David Elkind called the child of today "the hurried child." He believed that children are pushed to grow up too fast, pushed too hard to succeed in life, and not allowed to fully experience their childhoods.

38. A: A common point across differing definitions of culture is that culture is learned through socialization. Every profession defines culture in its own way. For our purposes, however, culture includes beliefs and behavior that are learned through socialization as well as being a group orientation.

39. C: Difficulty learning to read is a particular problem for hearing-impaired students, and many hearing-impaired people grow up in families in which other members do not learn sign language, and attend schools in which there are limited opportunities to interact with teachers and students who know how to use sign language. Frustration with not being able to communicate and with not catching verbal cues can make deaf people seem rude to others. Because Rose communicates fluently with her teacher, elective mutism and autistic disorders would be ruled out in this example.

40. A: A culture match enhances insight into the client's situation. A social worker of the same culture as the client can help to put the client at ease and also offer additional insight into the client's situation. However, being of the same culture does not ensure any greater level of counseling skill.

41. C: Stereotyping is often incorrect when addressing an entire group of people. Especially when applied to a whole group of people, stereotyping is often incorrect. Such blanket stereotyping is often subconscious, influencing one's choices even when one is unaware of doing it.

42. C: The social worker has not encountered clients from this culture before and has misinterpreted the client's lack of eye contact (or tact) and unwillingness to talk about himself (which would be rude in front of a strange professional woman). What she sees as a potential mental illness is in fact considered respectful manners in the client's culture—something the school counselor, with her familiarity of that culture, understood.

43. C: In working with minority groups, "situational control" refers to factors that influence the client's life. Regardless of how much control a client has over his or her choices, he or she still is influenced by situational factors, which should be considered in any counseling setting.

44. C: Acculturation refers to subordinate cultures emulating the dominant ones. Every society has one culture within it that is dominant. Subordinate cultures will sometimes attempt to emulate the dominant culture as a means of gaining greater acceptance within the society. Acculturation refers to such emulation and the degree to which an individual associates himself with the dominant culture.

45. D: When working with clients, professionals should keep in mind the words "known fasts" as a means to help combat stereotypes. Stereotyping can occur both consciously and subconsciously by professionals as well as non-professionals. By focusing on "known facts," a professional can maintain a clearer focus on a non-stereotypic mind-set.

46. C: In counseling situations, understanding behavioral cues can be necessary because of cultural diversity. Some studies suggest that body language can represent up to 75% of human communication. For this reason, and because cultural differences in behavioral expression are significant, a professional should be aware of cultural differences in nonverbal communication.

47. C: The older couple is reacting to the stress of sharing their home, and they have lost their way as a couple. The first actions are to address the couple's feeling that their marriage is in trouble and to help them remember how important it is—so important that they are asked to work on their marriage rather than focusing on the rest of the family. Helping this couple reestablish their solidarity in the onslaught of family members will help them undertake the rest of the problems as a pair working together, rather than turning against each other.

48. A: The client is exhibiting symptoms of a neurocognitive disorder. He is having cognitive changes without depressive symptoms. His cognitive symptoms have mildly diminished his activities of daily living, but he is able to complete them with modifications, indicating a mild neurocognitive disorder.

49. D: Neurocognitive disorders could be specified as being due to any of the following: Alzheimer's disease, frontotemporal lobar degeneration, Parkinson's disease, Huntington's disease, Lewy body disease, traumatic brain injury, vascular disease, HIV infection, Prion disease, substance use, multiple etiologies, or another medical condition.

50. B: Specifiers that are appropriate for ASD include severity (mild, moderate, severe, profound), with or without accompanying intellectual impairment, with or without accompanying language impairment, associated with other mental/behavioral/neurodevelopmental issues, associated with medical/genetic/environmental factors, associated with catatonia.

51. D: The Diagnostic and Statistical Manual of Mental Disorders was first published in 1952 by the American Psychiatric Association and has been revised several times since. The DSM-5 was released in 2013. It provides standard criteria for diagnosing mental disorders and, although attracting controversy from time to time, is still the standard used.

52. C: In cultural lag, people maintain the standards of their original culture, which may be inappropriate in the culture that they currently live. In this case, the father's patriarchal and domineering ways, normal to his cultural background, are accepted on one level as manifestations of his caring by his daughter, but they are also causing her distress because they limit her personal freedom.

53. D: Evidence-based practice and measurement (EBP) uses knowledge gained through research, combined with consumer values and clinical expertise, to make decisions about when and how to interact with clients. Evidence is gathered about what treatment may work best with particular clients and is administered appropriately.

54. B: Social workers tend to classify individuals through the person-in-environment (PIE) perspective, relating the client's level of functioning to biological, social, and psychological life issues.

55. A: According to the PIE perspective, environmental unresponsiveness is most likely to create social functioning disabilities. Transitions in life and relationship problems are two additional common person-in-environment (PIE) situations likely to cause social functioning difficulties.

56. D: Interviewing requires both learned and innate skills. Each interview conducted is unique. The social worker uses both learned information and innate skills to interact effectively with the client and achieve interview goals.

57. B: In the initial interview, it is best to ask a few direct questions as necessary in order to allay any feelings of vulnerability in the client. Because of the power differential that exists between client and social worker, clients often feel vulnerable in the initial interaction with a social worker. For this reason, excessive personal questions can lead to a client's feeling paranoid and anxious.

58. D: The therapist overtly helps the family formulate the problem, has each member speak, and brings covert communications into the open. She does not discuss the power issues in the family with the family members, but she can use what she observes to make further decisions about other interventions.

59. C: The onset of a substance abuse disorder typically occurs from late adolescence to early adulthood. An individual with a substance abuse disorder in adolescence is at risk for the disorder in adulthood as well.

60. A: Because of the high co-morbidity rate between substance abuse and other disorders, the social worker needs to look at any patterns of substance use by individuals who suffer from other disorders. Conversely, substance abuse may mask symptoms of other disorders.

61. B: People with borderline personality disorder exhibit variable moods and impulsive behavior along with a tendency to view others negatively. People with this disorder are very social yet have significant difficulty maintaining relationships.

62. C: Whereas the other three terms are designated as lack of motivation within the client, the theory of motivation-capacity-opportunity tends to view clients as willing to participate as long as the intervention is appropriate and as long as no external obstacles prevent the client from taking part in the process.

63. C: Manic episodes are commonly seen in bipolar disorder and are characterized by such factors as a decreased need for sleep, racing thoughts and unrealistic ideation. Criteria for a manic episode in adults are that the episode lasts most of the day for at least one week.

64. B: A first manic episode experienced after age forty is highly unlikely with bipolar disorder and more likely would be due to a medical condition or, perhaps, a substance abuse issue.

65. A: Bipolar disorder can easily be confused with borderline personality disorder. There is significant overlap between the symptoms of these two disorders, and the social worker must take care to differentiate between the two. Borderline personality disorder is characterized by interpersonal issues, while bipolar disorder is more likely to have a biological etiology.

66. D: The causes of many cases of early-onset intellectual disability are difficult to determine. However, major categories of risk include genetic conditions, problems during pregnancy (including at and after birth), poverty and cultural deprivation.

67. D: Bipolar disorder is primarily a mood disorder, while schizophrenia is characterized more by disordered thought patterns.

68. B: This is not an unusual situation: Even clients whose problems are wrecking their lives find it extremely difficult to change. In therapy, they may be labeled as "resistant" and "dumped," or conscientious helpers may struggle to suggest different solutions, only to find that nothing works— and to feel like they're failing the client. In this case, the social worker has done all she can and is working harder than her client (this is always a clue that something isn't right). She doesn't need to refer the client because he would probably act the same way with any helper. Jane's challenge is to stick with the client, to stop presenting him with solutions, and to wait until his problem becomes his problem again, not hers. If he is not motivated to change because his problem isn't causing him much suffering, he will drop out of therapy on his own. If the pressure on him has relaxed because he has shifted his responsibility for solving the problem to Jane, her relaxing of the hold on his problem will allow the pressure to rest on him again, which will eventually increase his motivation to change.

69. B: Thought insertion/withdrawal is a type of delusion and refers to the belief that thoughts are being put into or taken out of one's head.

70. B: Alzheimer's disease causes atrophy of the brain tissue and is the most common form of dementia. Cognitive deficits are a common result of this disease.

71. C: The paraphilia category of sexual disorders includes pedophilia, so it is the type of sexual disorder most likely to be brought to a social worker's attention.

72. C: Frotteurism is a type of paraphilia, or sexual disorder, in which an individual gains sexual enjoyment by touching genitalia to a non-consenting or unsuspecting individual.

73. D: Unlike major depressive disorder, which includes severe symptoms and lasts at least two weeks, dysthymic disorder has less intense symptoms and continues for two years or more.

74. B: Depression is the most common lifetime disorder. Some people may have one major episode, while others experience it as a recurring problem throughout their life.

75. D: Several factors can cause a person to be at a higher risk of attempting suicide, including having had thoughts about suicide in the past, a history of the behavior in one's family and a history of high mobility.

76. B: Freud believed that the pleasure principle was a human being's most basic need, and was one of the four forces that motivate behavior. The other three forces are anxiety, defense mechanisms and psychosexual development.

77. C: Freud divided the psyche into three parts—id, ego and superego—with the id being responsible for basic drives. Unable to take "no" for an answer, the id is ruled by the pleasure principle. In behaving like a child who insists on having his way, Richard is demonstrating the id in action.

78. B: Moral anxiety occurs when one acts contrary to his or her moral beliefs. In this case, the client had an abortion even though she is opposed to abortion. At least part of her anxiety is likely because she behaved counter to her belief system.

79. D: Rationalization is a defense mechanism. In this example, the client is repeatedly attempting to rationalize what has happened in an attempt to deal with her anxiety.

80. D: The protective level of care is that level required for children, the elderly, people with mental retardation, and people with disabilities. "Skilled" or "extended" care is usually associated with Medicaid designations for long-term nursing facilities. Intermediate care is a designation used for older people who cannot live alone but can manage activities of daily living and are not in need of full-time nursing care.

81. A: The genital stage lasts from age twelve until death. Freud believed that during this time people seek positive relationships that continue through career, family, etc.

82. D: The social worker is attempting to alter Patricia's problem behavior by bringing the subconscious into consciousness. Psychoanalytic therapy can modify behavior by helping the client deal with past memories and thus improve behavior. This is done by bringing the subconscious into conscious awareness, which aids in understanding the motivation for certain behaviors.

83. A: One way to modify a client's behavior through the use of psychoanalytic therapy is to strengthen the ego. In strengthening the ego, the social worker assists the client in the compromises between his moral issues (superego) and basic desires (id). Behavior is modified by an increased awareness of these issues.

84. B: With the therapeutic technique of free association, the client is instructed to quickly respond to whatever the social worker says without taking time to think about how he or she should respond. The use of free association is beneficial in gaining non-censored insight into a client's thoughts and feelings.

85. B: Perceptions are phenomenological aspects of the client. Gestalt therapy seeks to understand the perceptions of the client regarding behavior and its motivation.

86. D: While gestalt social workers recognize the significance of a client's past to behavior and attitudes, the greater emphasis is placed on the client's current thoughts, feelings and behavior.

87. C: Adlerian social workers seek to assist clients in moving toward their ideal self. This often is accomplished through re-education, which helps clients understand their goals and their place in the social order.

88. A: Albert Ellis felt that abnormal behavior resulted from irrational thinking and that the interpretation of life events, rather than the events themselves, causes an individual's choice of behavior. This is the basis of his rational emotive behavior therapy (REBT) approach.

89. D: This exemplifies person-centered therapy. Carl Rogers's person-centered therapy seeks to guide the client in finding his or her own way toward self-growth. Reflection, as demonstrated in the example, is a common Rogerian technique. It is crucial that a social worker possess the three key factors of positive regard, congruence and empathy, which are vital to the social worker-client relationship.

90. A: In the remedial model, the group acts as a means of change to assist individual goals. Unlike this clinically oriented approach, the reciprocal model works to assist both the individual and society (and the relationship between the two). Another common model is the social goals model, which is formed to meet social interests only.

91. C: Age is not often a significant factor with most groups. However, age may be a consideration in certain populations, such as among teenagers, where age has particular status.

92. A: The description of "open" or "closed" in regard to therapy groups refers to the timing of admission. Closed groups allow participation only by members chosen at the time the group is formed. Open groups allow people to join at any time.

93. B: This client may be described as undifferentiated. In Bowen family systems theory, "differentiation of self" is a major concept. Clients are either "differentiated" (indicating the ability to separate thoughts from feelings) or "undifferentiated" (unable to separate feelings from thoughts). In our example, the client is clearly undifferentiated.

94. D: The concept of family projection refers to a parent transferring his or her energies away from the conflicting spouse and onto a child within the family.

95. D: All of the examples would improve the statement of this treatment goal. In treatment planning, goals should be specific, realistic and measurable. It's not enough simply to state that a relationship needs to be improved. Goals should address specific ways to improve a relationship and should be realistic, specific and measurable (to determine progress).

96. A: The social worker is utilizing selective eclecticism. Selective eclecticism implies several possibilities but generally refers to blending more than one theory and/or being more open to treatment options. In this example, three types of therapy are represented—Rogerian, REBT and Freudian.

97. D: The four major steps of the casework process are study, assessment, intervention and termination. All of these steps work toward understanding what is dysfunctional and taking steps toward finding viable solutions.

98. B: The coleaders are trying to recruit "typical" students from the sciences—usually introverted, usually male—to balance out the outgoing female members. Whereas some groups are structured to meet the needs of a particular population (as in a group working on excessive shyness, in which everyone would be socially uncomfortable to some extent), others are built upon the idea that differences between members will enrich the experience for everyone. In such a group, leaders will seek variety in the group's members.

99. B: Modeling in therapy can be done in several ways but quite simply involves the client's imitating a particular interaction or behavior in order to replicate it.

100. D: This type of behavior is often termed "group cohesion" and refers to all the variables that keep a group together. When positive attributes outweigh the negative, the group members feel the attraction to stick together (or be cohesive). Cohesiveness is a healthy part of the group process.

101. B: The purpose of this activity is to make members comfortable in the group setting. In most new groups, the social worker has the responsibility to create a comfortable atmosphere conducive to free expression. A variety of exercises may be used to accomplish this, and such endeavors are sometimes referred to as "ice-breaker" exercises.

102. C: All aspects of the helping relationship depend upon communication. Beyond therapeutic skill, academic knowledge or other counseling-related factors, the basic ability to connect with another individual is a crucial first step.

103. C: Mark's history of violence in his intimate relationships and his current addictions to pornography and the internet, combined with his having PTSD and ADHD, produce a constellation of conditions that points to his having been abused as a child. He may well have been addicted to drugs or alcohol at an early age because it's not uncommon for abused children to turn to drugs to attempt to numb the pain and ease the memories of abuse, and current abuse or symptoms of PTSD will look like ADHD or learning disorders in the school setting. However, there is no current indication of drug or alcohol abuse.

104. A: Silence is a mode of communication that is often overlooked as a therapeutic tool. Many social workers often are uncomfortable with periods of silence and therefore are unable to make use of it in the treatment process. Anger can be useful as a therapeutic tool, but the social worker more often overlooks silence as an effective tool.

105. D: Clients can be nervous and confused in relating information during a therapy session. However, when the information being omitted is of significant relevance, it is more likely an issue of illogical thinking or even possible resistance to therapy.

106. C: A change in tone likely means that the client has significant emotional attachment to what is being said. At such times, the social worker should pay additional attention to what the client is saying and make a point to explore the situation.

107. A: It is significant to learn if a client takes responsibility for self or others because it is reflective of one's responsibility to resolve issues. Generally, blaming others for one's problems doesn't aid in fixing the problem. Neither is it productive for clients to act as martyrs and take responsibility for others' choices.

108. D: Empathy is often understood as feeling what another is feeling. However, in a therapeutic relationship, the social worker ideally does not feel, condone or identify with the client's feelings. An empathetic social worker seeks to understand a client's feelings and uses that understanding to assist the client.

109. B: Enabling behavior helps create situations in which the other person's dysfunction can continue. Enabling may take the form of providing the substance, but it may also happen when someone tries to deprive the addicted person of the substance, which gives that person cause for resentment and another "reason" to continue the destructive pattern.

110. A: A social worker should possess and exhibit self-confidence, which assists in setting boundaries and maintaining professional distance. Self-confidence also makes it less likely that the social worker will fall into the habit of trying to please the client rather than say what needs to be said.

111. D: An astute social worker must consider all of these possibilities in response to this client. While it's certainly a possibility that a client is lying in an interview, it is less likely than the possibility that he or she is either altering facts (to make discussing them more comfortable) or that the client's recollections of events may have altered over time.

112. B: When clients fail to return for treatment, social workers often overlook the possibility that the client's needs have been met. Instead, social workers are quick to label the client as resistant or to view their own skills as lacking in some way. Some clients, however, require only one session to feel their needs have been met.

113. C: The social worker is demonstrating being a good listener. Part of being an effective listener consists of asking questions. Assumptions regarding what's being said can be problematic, because communication can differ from person to person.

114. B: This should notify the social worker to focus attention on the issue of Jamie's mother. Even when a client is verbal and appears to be invested in honestly exploring significant issues, there often is some resistance to confronting the most pertinent (and painful) issues. Jamie's behavior is indicative of this type of situation.

115. C: Depression is strongly associated with addiction, and in many cases, it's difficult to discern which comes first. Some theories of addiction say that people become addicted in an attempt to self-medicate their long-standing and pervasive depression. In general, mental illness presents a risk for substance abuse as the patient attempts to self-medicate to overcome their struggles.

116. D: To listen with a third ear means to look for hidden meaning in what the client is communicating. Additional meaning may be gleaned from many factors beyond the actual spoken words, such as behavioral cues, tone of voice and more. In this example, Janet's hand movements and change in verbal tone are significant to what she is really thinking and feeling.

117. A: The "mistake of assumption" refers to accepting the presenting problem as the actual or only problem. Sometimes even the client is unaware of why he or she has come into counseling. Social workers should never assume that the reason stated for counseling is the actual or only issue to be addressed.

118. D: Setting strict boundaries on availability is an important element of the professional relationship between social worker and client. It is important that a social worker be available to the client. This means not, however, that the social worker should always be available, but rather that he or she should be reachable within a reasonable amount of time. Availability becomes a "double-edged sword" when some clients become unreasonably dependent upon the social worker and such contact inhibits their ability to act independently.

119. D: It's a common mistake to assume only one or two of the most obvious underlying feelings when it comes to statements made by clients. Consideration must be given to the wide range of feelings possible within one simple statement. In this example, it's obvious (by the tearfulness of the client) that the comment is highly charged emotionally and likely holds a depth of feeling.

120. C: This client/ social worker interaction could be improved in several ways. The first comment is shallow and does not address the feelings presented. The second comment would have better included a more descriptive word, such as "frustrated" or "furious." The final statement gives inappropriate reassurance of what will happen in the course of therapy, which the social worker has no right to ensure.

121. C: This type of behavior is sometimes referred to as "disqualifying communication," meaning that, by words or actions, it disqualifies what one has just said. In the example, the client makes a comment about liking his job and respecting his brother. However, his use of the words "lousy" and "idiot" run counter to the meaning behind those statements and thus disqualify what appears to be the intended message.

122. C: This exchange hints that Bob is dominating in the relationship. In every communication between two people, a message is apparent in the content of what is spoken, but information also is conveyed about the feelings present and the relationship between the two parties involved. In this case, the relationship message inherent in what is said indicates that Bob is dominant, doing what he chooses, with Jan requesting to be treated differently.

123. B: Communication is sometimes referred to as a circular reciprocally interacting process. In communication, each interaction is a consequence of the interaction that preceded it, and the receiver of a message becomes the sender of the next one. Around and around it goes in a continuing loop.

124. C: Because this young man's withdrawn behavior has been persistent throughout his lifespan, he would most likely be considered to have a schizoid personality. (Because he is at the age dividing adolescence from adulthood in the diagnostic criterion, without evidence that his behavior has been lifelong, he might have been diagnosed with schizoid disorder of adolescence.) Schizophreniform disorder is much less adaptive and contains features of schizophrenia, and although someone might be considered to have a highly introverted personality, introversion is not a diagnosable condition.

125. B: While it may be prudent for a social worker to speak with a supervisor or colleague about what he or she is experiencing, the best first step would be self-examination. Self-awareness is an important quality in a competent social worker, which is why social workers often are urged to enter counseling themselves. It's important for a social worker to be self-aware in order to competently treat clients.

126. D: Counseling can be interminable when factors exist that limit its ability to be effective. One of those factors is when therapy goals are unrealistic. In this case, the goal of never experiencing conflict when making decisions is an unrealistic one, so counseling is likely to be interminable unless the error is noted and corrected.

127. A: The social worker should take a position of extreme caution. Suicidal clients who suddenly feel better are often not improving but rather are less conflicted because they have made the decision to take their lives. This is when extreme caution should be exercised by the social worker, because the risk to the client is actually higher.

128. C: Transference is likely causing the client's feelings. Transference is a Freudian term that describes a client's placing feelings for another onto the social worker. In this case, especially because of the problematic relationship issues, the client is likely to be transferring feelings inaccurately onto the social worker.

129. A: The NASW specifies ethical principles based on the values that should guide all social workers. "The value of service" refers to the ethical principle of helping those in need and addressing social issues. Social workers are expected to use their skills to serve others and even donate some of their time in such service.

130. B: The NASW's ethical principle of social justice specifies that all social workers should work toward social change, especially for those in particular need. They also should seek to improve awareness and sensitivity about social issues.

131. A: Social workers are expected to respect the dignity and worth of every person, which is a value specified by the NASW.

132. C: The importance of human relationships is recognized by social workers, and the connection between these relationships is a focus of the social worker's professional practice.

133. A: Anorexia has been associated with cultural pressures that result in body image distortions and attempts to control perceived weight gain. Although it certainly has neurobiological concomitance, its cause has not been identified as organic.

134. A: Social workers are expected to respect a client's right to self-determination. However, if a client's choice of action threatens himself or the welfare of others, a social worker may limit that right.

135. B: A social worker is ethically responsible to practice only within those areas where he or she is competent. Because the client's welfare must be paramount, the social worker in this case should not discontinue counseling but should consult with someone who is competent in psychosis and proceed from there.

136. C: Yes, this situation may present a dual relationship that can create a conflict of interest. Conflicts of interest are not ethically allowed in counseling relationships and are to be avoided.

137. A: The social worker must explicitly discuss the limits of confidentiality with this particular client. Confidentiality is a critical issue in social work, but there are limits, and a client should be made aware of those limits. In this case, suicide ideation may present a situation where confidentiality needs to be breached. To ensure a positive client/ social worker relationship, the client should be made particularly aware of confidentiality limits.

138. B: Social workers have a responsibility to provide clients with their records upon request. In some cases, however, interpretation may be needed. Also, social workers should be careful that the confidentiality of other people's material in an individual's records is protected.

139. D: The social worker should refer this client to another social worker. It is not considered ethically responsible to enter into a counseling relationship with someone with whom the social worker previously had a sexual relationship. Professional boundaries are difficult to maintain in this situation, and harm to the client could ensue.

140. D: Before engaging in physical contact with a client, the social worker should take into account the possible psychological, social and cultural ramifications of such contact. Taking a client's hand or a pat on the back can be interpreted differently depending upon the client and situation. Clear boundaries should be set for such conduct.

141. C: Many of the elderly are overmedicated or are taking medications whose interaction effects create additional ailments, such as headaches, confusion, and emotional problems. In a medication review, each medication is considered in relation to the others, and a review may discover that medications from different doctors or for different illnesses are causing new problems for the client.

142. A: The counselor should terminate both counseling and the relationship, and refer the client to a colleague. It's not ethically permissible to enter into a sexual relationship with past or present clients. If an unprofessional relationship is forming and boundaries cannot be maintained, then the client should be referred out and the relationship terminated.

143. C: If a colleague is known to be practicing in an incompetent manner, that colleague should be met with and steps taken to assist in bringing him or her up to a competent level. If this is not effective, then action should be taken to address the problem through appropriate channels.

144. A: According to the NASW, social workers are ethically obligated to help during times of social emergencies and to do so to the greatest extent possible. There is no specification as to how best to assist.

145. B: Researchers ethically must inform research subjects of all the risks and benefits of study participation. Informed, written consent should be obtained, without inducement.

146. C: Regarding models of authority in social work settings, two basic types of supervisors often are chosen, based either on authority or on competence. The authority model suggests that supervisors are chosen based upon their position in the organization's hierarchical structure. The competence model implies that an individual performs a supervisory role because of specific training and experience.

147. A: In the peer supervision model, all members participate equally. They are responsible for their own work but meet periodically to share experiences and offer professional advice on each other's cases.

148. B: Autonomous work refers to social workers performing their duties independently, without the need for formal supervision of their work. Some believe that this self-directed approach to practice is better because it doesn't stifle creativity.

149. B: The supervisory-function model of supervision takes into account three specific areas of supervision, which are administrative, educational and supportive. In this case, the supervisor is addressing all three areas of concern in providing supervisory services.

150. D: An ideal supervisory situation includes "shared meaning." This refers to when the supervisor and supervisee achieve mutual understanding and agreement on the issues reviewed. If shared meaning is high, then the effectiveness of the supervision interaction also will be high.

151. B: Sample generalization underlies this view of research. Generalizability refers to the extent that research can tell us about people or things that were not actually studied. In this case, survivors of sexual assault are studied in a crisis center, and then the information gathered is generalized to apply to all assault survivors. This is sample generalization because not all assault survivors are being studied but only the small sample that come to the crisis center.

152. D: Quantitative method tends to involve findings that are numerical in nature. Qualitative methods are more likely to include narratives and observations.

153. D: In the team service-delivery approach, all team members share in the responsibility for making decisions about the services offered. However, there is a team leader who acts as a supervisor, and whenever there is dissent among the members, the team leader has the final say.

154. A: Trust is critical to a successful supervisor/supervisee relationship because the supervisee must feel secure in revealing what is happening with his clients, as well as in describing his own thoughts and feelings.

155. D: Policy often is created through a series of repeated steps. It begins with the identification of a problem and then proceeds through goal-setting formulation, implementation, evaluation, change and, finally, termination.

156. A: Social workers that understand policy and recognize the barriers clients may face receiving services tend to be effective at maximizing clients' access to benefits. Part of a social worker's role is to understand policy and recognize barriers to clients' receiving services so that alternatives to those barriers can be found.

157. D: Clients generally prefer to be involved in the decision-making process when it comes to receiving services. However, those who are intellectually impaired, for instance those suffering from dementia, low IQ, or head injury, may prefer to have direction provided for them.

158. C: The type of service delivery determined by the provider is often called "provider-driven." In consumer-driven care, the consumer takes the active role in determining what services are wanted and offered.

159. D: Measuring service delivery is necessary in order to manage economic factors and to increase the efficiency and effectiveness of the services provided.

160. C: The three E's include effort, efficiency and effectiveness. "Effort" refers to the resources used in carrying out the program. How well the program uses those resources to reach its intended results speaks to "efficiency." Finally, "effectiveness" refers to how well the goals of the program were reached.

161. C: After her work became famous, Kubler-Ross was dismayed that practitioners and lay readers conceptualized the stages in a linear fashion, when in fact, the grief process can involve cycling back to earlier stages over longer periods of time.

162. B: Record-keeping is a critical component of professional social work management. Maintaining appropriate records has the obvious benefit of creating a history of treatment of the individual client; however, there are other advantages as well. Good record-keeping is increasingly important because it often influences funding and also provides justification for services provided. The record also may be useful in research and in improving future services.

163. A: Process recording is sometimes used in cases in educational settings or those involving the courts or legal issues. It is useful in the training of social work students but is often felt to be too involved, cumbersome and time-consuming in everyday practice. Process recording includes a face sheet, contracts, client interpretations, and in-depth contact information for everyone involved in treatment.

164. D: Audio and/or videotaping as a case-based recording is often used in medical situations and as a way to train students or staff in educational settings. This approach is almost always used in conjunction with supplemental record-keeping.

165. D: SOAP refers to problem-oriented recording. Just as it sounds, problem-oriented recording involves a statement of the problem and when it was resolved. This type of approach is commonly used in the medical setting, with SOAP (subjective-objective-assessment-plan) as the guideline for charting the client's treatment. "S" is information relative to the client's request. "O" refers to the observable and measurable criteria. "A" is the social worker's assessment, and "P" notes how treatment will be carried out.

166. C: GAS may help by providing specific measurement of treatment goals." GAS (goal attainment scaling) is a well-respected tool used for measuring program treatment outcomes. It is a client-specific technique that links treatment goals and outcomes with scaled points, making for a flexible evaluation tool.

167. A: The medical model may be causing the discord in this situation. Social workers often come into contact with nurses and other professionals, and it is not uncommon for two separate but related professions to clash. Nurses are trained in the medical model, seeing the consumer as a patient and viewing services in a very concrete, authoritarian manner. Social workers view the person as a client, as someone who will take an active role in determining his own treatment, and they more often act as an advocate for the client. These differences in orientation can sometimes lead to professional conflict.

168. D: The best question to ask to determine any other ways in which the client medicates himself is, "What do you do to relieve pain when you have a headache?" When taking a medication history, one should include the type of medication, patterns of use and potential for abuse. However, a client may medicate himself in many ways. It's important to ask about such things as alcohol, caffeine and nicotine, but one is far more likely to obtain valuable information about less obvious self-treatments (such as herbal remedies or supplements) by keeping the question more open-ended.

169. B: Community-based practice refers to locating services in the place where the population to be served actually lives. There are significant benefits to providing services in this way, including the likelihood that members of the community will support the organization in their own community. Clients who have easier access to services and feel more comfortable in familiar surroundings also are more likely to make use of the services offered.

170. D: It's not all that unusual for prior clients to turn up in later years as volunteers or social workers themselves. Sometimes they may even turn up as colleagues working in the same facility. A social worker must decide, on a case-by-case basis, if the past relationship was such that he or she can work professionally with the past client. In some cases it may be permissible; in others it clearly will not work. In either case, a social worker should make his or her supervisor aware of the situation.

Practice Test #2

1. The fundamental premise of Freud's psychoanalytic theory is that human behavior is best understood as arising from:

   a. social constraints and mores.
   b. drives and unconscious motivations.
   c. instinct and physiological needs.
   d. a desire for power and control.

2. Distressing and anxiety-provoking thoughts may be rejected by the conscious mind and forced into the unconscious mind by a process called:

   a. reaction formation.
   b. denial.
   c. transference.
   d. repression.

3. According to Freud's structural theory of personality development, mental disturbances and psychological maladjustments are primarily the result of:

   a. cognitive dissonance.
   b. defense mechanisms.
   c. conflicts between the id, ego, and superego.
   d. neuroses.

4. Maria is raising her two children alone, working full time, and caring for her mother, who has recently started wandering away from the house and becoming lost. Maria has started experiencing bouts of anger, followed by apathy. She feels she has more responsibility than she can handle and that she has little control over the financial and physical safety of her family. She continues being a responsible employee and a nurturing caregiver, but she is feeling the pressure. What is the most correct term for Maria's problem?

   a. Existential crisis.
   b. Identity crisis.
   c. Burnout.
   d. Generalized anxiety.

5. Freud's psychoanalytic theory incorporated the structural theory of personality development. Freud believed that personality development is completed by:

   a. 5 years of age.
   b. 3 years of age.
   c. 7 years of age.
   d. 6 years of age.

6. The Freudian terms cathexis and anti-cathexis refer to forces collectively known as:

   a. cognitive forces.
   b. developmental forces.
   c. primary forces.
   d. driving forces.

7. How can a social worker best begin work with a client so that both parties have clear expectations of the goals, the time period the work will cover, and each one's responsibilities in the working relationship?

 a. By having an implicit understanding naturally arise during the work
 b. By discussing and writing goals, processes, and timetables at the beginning of the counseling work and reevaluating priorities at regular intervals
 c. By discussing goals, processes, and timetables as the work proceeds
 d. By reviewing together what's been achieved at the end of treatment

8. Each of Freud's five stages of psychosexual development is associated with certain age ranges. The phallic stage typically occurs during which age range?

 a. 2-4 years of age
 b. 5-9 years of age
 c. 3-6 years of age
 d. 7-14 years of age

9. The theory of defense mechanisms was developed by:

 a. Sigmund Freud.
 b. Erik Erikson.
 c. Heinz Hartmann.
 d. Anna Freud.

10. The defense mechanism known as reaction formation is best described as:

 a. a psychological response to an internal conflict.
 b. substituting an opposite response to relieve distress.
 c. going to the opposite extreme to resolve distress.
 d. overcompensation for unacceptable impulses.

11. The defense mechanism known as splitting is best described as:

 a. suppressing the contradictory qualities of a given entity or situation.
 b. dissociating difficult feelings that impair psychic well-being.
 c. disengaging emotions that cannot be reconciled.
 d. fragmentation of the self to reconcile conflicting feelings.

12. According to Heinz Hartmann's ego psychology, the terms alloplastic behavior and autoplastic behavior refer to aspects of:

 a. autonomy.
 b. regulation.
 c. adaptation.
 d. judgment.

13. One way that Heinz Hartmann's ego psychology differed from Sigmund Freud's views on personality structure was his view that:

 a. early experiences are more important than current environmental influence.
 b. parts of the personality must be integrated to solve conflict.
 c. defense mechanisms arise from the id not the ego.
 d. children are born with both ids and egos.

14. One of the following dyads does not refer to the first six ego functions, as identified via ego psychology. Which of the following is the erroneously included dyad?

a. Judgment, regulation and control over drives and impulses
b. Idealization, intellectualization
c. Sense of reality, reality testing
d. Thought processes, object relations

15. One of the following dyads does not refer to a second group of six ego functions, as identified via ego psychology. Which of the following is the erroneously included dyad?

a. Autonomous functions, integrative functioning
b. Stimulus barrier, mastery-competence
c. Defensive functioning, adaptive regression
d. Displacement, substitution

16. Which one of the following did not principally contribute to object relations?

a. Carl Jung
b. Rene Spitz
c. Margaret Mahler
d. John Bowlby

17. Mahler's symbiotic stage of development occurs during which of the following months of infant life?

a. 1 to 5 months after birth
b. Between birth and 1month of age
c. 14 to 24 months after birth
d. 9 to 14 months after birth

18. A key difference between self-psychology and object relations theory is its focus on:

a. an empathic environment.
b. object constancy.
c. individuation of the self from others.
d. the self/self-object relationship.

19. Of the following, which is the best definition of empathic mirroring?

a. A self-object that responds in nurturing ways
b. An internal self-validation that affirms self-worth
c. An empathic process by which the self-object fully accepts the embryonic grandiose self
d. The bond between the self and the self-object that serves to sustain the self during times of distress

20. In self-psychology, the process by which positive objects are integrated into an internalized self-structure is known as:

a. self-object integration.
b. transmuting internalization.
c. self/self-object fusion.
d. normative self-aggregation.

21. Fritz Perls' gestalt theory differs from Freud's psychoanalytic theory in all but which of the following ways?
  a. Issues and problems are integral to personal experiences
  b. Behavior is not driven by unconscious drives
  c. Personality development is idiosyncratic, not "step-wise"
  d. Actions are conscious and immediately controllable

22. Which theorist is one of the earliest to address human development from a total lifespan perspective?
  a. Alfred Adler
  b. Jean Piaget
  c. Erik Erikson
  d. Lawrence Kohlberg

23. Erikson's terms syntonic and dystonic, as used in psychosocial theory, are best defined with which of the following less technical words?
  a. Loose versus taut
  b. Calm versus anxious
  c. Relaxed versus rigid
  d. Positive versus negative

24. In Erikson's psychosocial stages of development the stage of autonomy versus shame and doubt occurs between which of the following ages?
  a. Birth to 1 year of age
  b. 2 to 3 years of age
  c. 4 to 5 years of age
  d. 6 to 11 years of age

25. Although Sophie doesn't ignore the fact that her client has a gambling addiction and bipolar personality disorder, in sessions, she focuses on his skill at calculating statistics and his love of animals. Which perspective is Sophie operating from with this client?
  a. A strengths-based perspective
  b. A solution-focused perspective
  c. A structural perspective
  d. A behavioral perspective

26. Developmentally, the capacity to throw objects and walk backwards and sideways emerges during which age range?
  a. 6-8 months of age
  b. 9-12 months of age
  c. 15-17 months of age
  d. 18-19 months of age

27. Differences in motor skills between males and females become most evident during which age range?
  a. 7-11 years of age
  b. 12-15 years of age
  c. 16-18 years of age
  d. 18-30 years of age

28. The term schemas, according to Jean Piaget, is used to refer to:
   a. environmental circumstances.
   b. goal-oriented strategies for learning.
   c. concepts of moral development.
   d. situational responses to stimuli.

29. According to Piaget, a child begins to use symbols (i.e., language, images, etc.) during which developmental stage?
   a. Sensorimotor
   b. Pre-Operational
   c. Concrete Operational
   d. Formal Operational

30. According to Piaget, a child develops the capacity for abstract thinking during which developmental stage?
   a. Formal operational
   b. Sensorimotor
   c. Pre-operational
   d. Concrete operational

31. The two most prominent cognitive theorists from other theorists presented below are:
   a. Fritz Perls and Erik Erikson.
   b. Lawrence Kohlberg and Albert Bandura.
   c. Alfred Adler and Albert Ellis.
   d. John Watson and Ivan Pavlov.

32. What is another name for rational emotive therapy (RET)?
   a. Cognitive conscious therapy
   b. Reality therapy
   c. Logotherapy
   d. The ABC theory of emotion

33. Lawrence Kohlberg's theory of moral development was an extension of:
   a. Erik Erikson's psychosocial theory.
   b. Jean Piaget's theory of cognitive development.
   c. Fritz Perl's gestalt psychology.
   d. Sigmund Freud's psychoanalytic theory.

34. Lawrence Kohlberg proposed multiple levels and stages to moral development, specifically:
   a. three levels with two stages in each level.
   b. two levels with three stages in each level.
   c. three levels with three stages in each level.
   d. four levels with three stages in each.

35. An example of negative reinforcement is:
   a. the application of an uncomfortable stimulus.
   b. removal of an adverse stimulus following a positive behavior.
   c. a specific treat for avoiding negative behavior.
   d. an adverse stimulus for failing to behave positively.

36. Classical conditioning theory is also known as:
   a. consequence conditioning theory.
   b. stimulus conditioning theory.
   c. respondent conditioning theory.
   d. reinforcement conditioning theory.

37. According to Albert Bandura's social learning theory, an antecedent event is best described as:
   a. an expected consequence of a specific stimulus.
   b. a planned behavior leading to an expected outcome.
   c. a pre-determined stimulus that precipitates a behavioral event.
   d. an external event occurring immediately prior to a specific behavior.

38. Minority groups are best described as:
   a. any collection of individuals who feel marginalized.
   b. individuals recognized as having uniquely identifiable characteristics.
   c. individuals harassed or oppressed by others.
   d. a subset of individuals with differing characteristics.

39. The National Association of Social Workers (NASW) Standards for Cultural Competence indicate that the most important need for self-awareness in matters of diversity is:
   a. to determine one's own minority or majority status.
   b. to better appreciate the beliefs and cultural values of others.
   c. to accurately identify differences between oneself and others.
   d. to celebrate one's own unique values and beliefs.

40. Kay is leading a group focused on expressing their feelings and needs, and standing up for their rights and beliefs. Which coping skill is being addressed MOST especially in the group?
   a. Assertiveness
   b. Positive thinking
   c. Healthy communication
   d. Stress reduction

41. According to the NASW, the policies, behaviors, and attitudes to work well with people regardless of race, religion, class, or culture is formally referred to as:
   a. diversity capacity.
   b. cultural proficiency.
   c. cultural competence.
   d. diversity awareness.

42. Which one of the following is NOT a key to developing a culturally competent practice?
   a. Become self-aware of personal beliefs and values
   b. Treat others as one desires to be treated
   c. Learn about the cultures of those served in the practice
   d. Discover one's cultural knowledge limits

43. A newly immigrated individual from Asia refuses to hear the risks and benefits of a proposed procedure, and insists that the physician let her husband decide. The physician should:
   a. refuse to consider the procedure citing lack of informed consent.
   b. demand that the patient listen and bring in an interpreter to tell her.
   c. do the procedure as needed without talking to anyone.
   d. follow the patient's wishes and inform the husband.

44. A social worker becomes aware of certain abusive child disciplinary practices in a family that are nevertheless commonplace in that family's culture. The social worker should:
   a. report the behavior to a designated child protective agency.
   b. dismiss the behavior because it is normative in that culture.
   c. seek assurances from the family that they will stop the practice.
   d. ask the child if they feel the discipline is acceptable or not.

45. Having strong negative feelings or disparaging thoughts about others based solely on differences due to disabilities, age, gender orientation, poverty, education, race, religion, culture, ethnicity, and language is best defined as being:
   a. prejudiced.
   b. biased.
   c. discriminatory.
   d. judgmental.

46. Which of the following does not represent a common minority classification?
   a. Age
   b. Race
   c. Religion
   d. Gender

47. Feelings and beliefs that one's own ethnic group or culture is superior to all others is referred to as:
   a. egocentrism.
   b. multiculturalism.
   c. cultural narcissism.
   d. ethnocentrism.

48. The first stage of treatment is generally agreed to be:
   a. treatment plan formulation.
   b. assessment.
   c. clinical diagnosis.
   d. contracting.

49. In anger management training, which technique includes getting a different perspective on the situation?

    a. Relaxation
    b. Communication
    c. Cognition
    d. Environmental change

50. A social assessment report should NOT include:

    a. medical records.
    b. demographic facts.
    c. social data.
    d. social work data assessment and interpretation.

51. Genograms and ecomaps are used to structure and explore a client's:

    a. genetic and health history.
    b. income and economic resources.
    c. generative and gravida histories.
    d. family and social relationships.

52. A 21-year-old female presents as despondent and distressed after a break-up with her boyfriend. She discloses that she has been contemplating "ending it all" and notes that she has researched ways to end her life on the internet. When asked, she reveals that she has collected some, but not all, of the materials necessary for a painless suicide. The social worker's best response to this information would be to:

    a. explore the client's level of intent to take further action.
    b. arrange for hospitalization immediately.
    c. enter into a "no-suicide contract" with the patient.
    d. have the client immediately call the local suicide hotline.

53. A home health social worker sees a 72-year-old home-bound client who is depressed over the recent death of his wife and expresses significant suicidal feelings. He later verbally agrees to a no-suicide contract but refuses to sign a written agreement, saying that his word should be good enough. The social worker's best response would be to:

    a. arrange for psychiatric hospitalization.
    b. call a relative to come be with the client.
    c. arrange a next-day follow-up visit.
    d. accept his verbal assurance.

54. During a family counseling session, a social worker notices that when the mother raises her arm for any reason her nearby child flinches and starts to pull back. The social worker should evaluate the child for evidence of:

    a. psychological abuse.
    b. emotional abuse.
    c. physical abuse.
    d. sexual abuse.

55. A male school social worker meets with a grade-school girl who repeatedly asks if the social worker thinks she is cute, if he wants to kiss or hug her, and who is dressed rather provocatively. The social worker should suspect:

    a. psychological abuse.
    b. emotional abuse.
    c. physical abuse.
    d. sexual abuse.

56. Which is the most commonly used Intelligence Quotient (IQ) test in the United States?

    a. Stanford-Binet Intelligence Scale, fifth version (SB5)
    b. Wechsler Adult Intelligence Scale (WAIS)
    c. Implicit Theory of Intelligence Scale (ITIS)
    d. Personal Conception of Intelligence Scale (PCIS)

57. The precursor to the Diagnostic and Statistical Manual of Mental Disorders (DSM) was the:

    a. Catalogue of Neuroses and Psychiatric Disease.
    b. Manual of Abnormal Psychiatry.
    c. Compendium of Psychiatric Disorders.
    d. International Classification of Diseases.

58. A 40-year-old client presents with complaints regarding not feeling comfortable socially. He states that after gaining weight he now finds social situations to be overwhelming. He has stopped attending church and recreational activities, and does not engage in new activities, although before he was known for being adventurous. A likely diagnosis would be:

    a. borderline personality disorder.
    b. avoidant personality disorder.
    c. schizotypal personality disorder.
    d. depressive disorder.

59. The DSM-5 provides for the diagnosis of specific personality disorders and one category for indeterminate behaviors that appear to be characteristic of a personality disorder. These disorders are grouped into clusters. Which of the following clusters does not properly describe a personality disorder group?

    a. Cluster A: paranoid, schizoid, and schizotypal disorders (also referred to as "odd or eccentric behavior disorders")
    b. Cluster B: impulsivity and/or affective dysregulation disorders (also referred to as "dramatic, emotional, or erratic disorders")
    c. Cluster C: anxiety and compulsive disorders (also referred to as "anxious or fearful disorders")
    d. Cluster D: violent and/or explosive disorders (also referred to as "aggressive and intrusive conduct disorders")

60. Certain DSM-5 codes are used to identify conditions that are a focus of clinical attention, but for which insufficient information exists to determine if the issues can be attributed to a mental disorder (or which may, in fact, not be due to a mental disorder but still require clinical attention). These codes are called:
   a. DSM-5 Codes.
   b. GAF Codes.
   c. V Codes.
   d. ICD Codes.

61. A client comes to see a social worker with numerous personal issues of varying severity. The decision regarding the issue(s) that should be addressed first should be made:
   a. by the client alone.
   b. by the client, in exploration with the social worker.
   c. by the social worker alone.
   d. based upon severity of life impact.

62. A social worker has been seeing a client for several weeks, with considerable progress having been made. As a mutually agreed upon date for termination approaches, the client expresses considerable anxiety and even some anger regarding the impending termination. The social worker's best initial response would be to do which of the following?
   a. Offer a follow-up appointment some weeks away
   b. Assure the client that services can again be sought at any time
   c. Cancel the termination date and continue services
   d. Explore and discuss the client's feelings about termination

63. According the DSM-5 criteria, a client that has previously met the criteria for stimulant use disorder but now has not met the criteria for stimulant use in 10 months (except for craving) would be termed to be in _____ remission.
   a. full
   b. partial
   c. early
   d. sustained

64. A 19-year-old college student sustains a severe head injury in an accident. Post-rehab testing reveals a subsequent IQ of 62. Which diagnosis would be the most likely?
   a. Dementia, mild, due to head trauma
   b. Mild neurocognitive disorder due to traumatic brain injury
   c. Borderline intellectual functioning
   d. Intellectual disability, mild, due to head trauma

65. A single mother and a teenage son present for relationship problems. The son is actively defiant of instructions, argues regularly over minor requests, and can be spiteful and resentful over normal parenting efforts. School performance is marginal, but only one unexcused absence has occurred during the current school year, which is nearing its end. The most appropriate diagnosis would be:
   a. oppositional defiant disorder.
   b. conduct disorder.
   c. intermittent explosive disorder.
   d. parent-child relational problem.

66. An elderly female client presents with marked disorientation, word-finding problems, memory impairment, and a high degree of distractibility. Her daughter states that the patient was "just fine" until two days prior to this contact, and that she seems better in the mornings. There have been no external or environmental changes. The most likely diagnosis would be:

    a. medication-induced cognitive changes.
    b. senile dementia, rapid onset.
    c. delirium.
    d. neurocognitive disorder, not otherwise specified.

67. A husband and wife present for help with her substance use. She had been recreationally using cocaine on some weekends, and indicates that she has a strong desire to stop, but has been unsuccessful in stopping before. The precipitating incident was an episode of driving under the influence on a weeknight that resulted in her arrest, impounding of the family car, and considerable fines, charges, and increases in automobile insurance. This is the second driving incident in the last two years. The most appropriate diagnosis for the wife, given the relevant details would be:

    a. stimulant intoxication.
    b. stimulant dependence.
    c. stimulant use disorder.
    d. stimulant use withdrawal.

68. A 20-year-old male college student has been referred for evaluation by his family. They note that over the last six to seven months he has increasingly avoided contact and/or talking with family members and friends, that he often seems intensely preoccupied, and that his hygiene and grooming have become very poor. In speaking with him the social worker notes that he seems very guarded, that his affect is virtually expressionless, and that he resists talking. When the social worker is able to coax him to speak, his speech is very tangential, disorganized, and even incoherent at times. He seems to be responding to internal stimuli (hallucinations and/or intrusive thoughts). The family and he deny substance abuse. Which would be the MOST likely diagnosis?

    a. Schizophrenia
    b. Somatization disorder
    c. Bipolar disorder
    d. Major depression with psychotic features

69. A 56-year-old man presents with personal problems. Two months ago, he lost his job, following which he reports feeling depressed most days. He acknowledges increased alcohol consumption, and that he cannot seem to enjoy doing anything, not even golf, which he used to love. He feels useless, empty, and helpless, and he has gained over 18 lbs. Then he adds, "Sometimes I hear voices telling me I'm just 'no good,' and that things will never get better. Only booze seems to get the voices to stop. Do you think I'm going crazy?" What would be the client's most likely primary diagnosis?

    a. Alcohol-induced mood disorder
    b. Alcohol-induced psychotic disorder, with auditory hallucinations
    c. Major depression with psychotic features
    d. Major depression

55

70. **A 22-year-old college student comes to a hospital emergency room complaining of chest pain. The medical work-up is negative. The social worker learns that his father recently died of a heart attack (a few weeks ago) while he was away at school, and that he is now experiencing episodes of sudden-onset fear accompanied by symptoms such as a rapid heart rate, sweating, tremors, chest pain, and shortness of breath, and feelings that he is about to die. After a short time, the symptoms subside. In recent days he has been sleeping outside the hospital, fearful that he may not otherwise arrive in time when the symptoms strike. Which is the most likely diagnosis?**

    a. Generalized anxiety disorder
    b. Panic disorder
    c. Somatization disorder
    d. Post-traumatic stress disorder

71. **Bipolar disorder is most commonly treated with which of the following medication?**

    a. Lithium
    b. Haloperidol
    c. Librium
    d. Prozac

72. **A 48-year-old woman is seen in clinic for personal problems. Upon interview she describes having quit her grocery clerk job because of fear that something might happen that she can't cope with at the work site. When pressed, she is vague but finally states that she's fearful she could have gas (burping or flatulence), bowel or bladder incontinence, or be badly embarrassed by others on the job. She acknowledges that she has no current gaseous or incontinence issues, and that she's never been humiliated by anyone in the past. However, she insists that she cannot tolerate the possibility it might occur. The most likely diagnosis is:**

    a. panic disorder.
    b. agoraphobia.
    c. social anxiety disorder.
    d. general anxiety disorder.

73. **As part of a pending disability application, a social worker meets with the client. The client voices complaints about significant chronic back and shoulder pain, which is the basis of the claim. During the course of the in-home assessment the social worker notes that the individual is able to bend down to move and pick things up, and is able to reach over her head into an upper cabinet—all without apparent difficulty or complaints of pain. The most appropriate determination would be:**

    a. illness anxiety disorder.
    b. malingering.
    c. factitious disorder.
    d. somatic symptom disorder.

74. A couple presents for counseling. Evaluation reveals that the wife comes from a dysfunctional, neglectful, alcoholic home and has little trust or tolerance for relationships. Consequently, their marriage is marred by constant arguing and distrust, frequent demands that he leave, episodes of impulsive violence, alternating with brief periods of excessive over-valuation (stating that he is the "best thing that ever happened" to her, "too good" for her, et cetera. Which is the most likely diagnosis?
   a. Anti-social personality disorder
   b. Histrionic personality disorder
   c. Borderline personality disorder
   d. Narcissistic personality disorder

75. A social worker should choose a practice framework based upon any of the following criteria EXCEPT:
   a. an accepted psychological theoretical base.
   b. treatment goals and treatment type (individual, family, group, etc.).
   c. the model most commonly used by other social workers.
   d. the client's problem and/or time and resources available.

76. Which one of the following do NOT represent common practice frameworks?
   a. Ethnic-sensitive and feminist frameworks
   b. Systems and eco-system frameworks
   c. Generalist and strengths frameworks
   d. Behavioral and cognitive frameworks

77. A newly divorced client has been working on numerous past marital issues, and was readily disclosing many feelings and concerns. However, when episodes of her infidelity arose, the client became reluctant to reveal her feelings about what had occurred, when, and its specific impact on her life. The psychoanalytic approach would refer to this as resistance and the proper response would be to:
   a. ignore the resistance in deference to the client's feelings.
   b. mention the resistance, but make no effort to move the client forward on the matter.
   c. confront the issue of resistance and make a point of addressing and exploring it with the client.
   d. require the client to continue disclosing her feelings and coping with her pain as related to this highly sensitive matter.

78. Which DSM-5 resource helps social workers clarify the impact of culture on clients' symptoms and possible treatment options?
   a. The list of culture-bound syndromes
   b. The cultural assimilation interview
   c. The cultural formulation interview guide
   d. The assessment of cultural deprivation

79. Key principles and concepts of the psychoanalytic approach include all of the following EXCEPT:

    a. individuals are best understood through their social environment.
    b. treatment is, by design, a short-term process, not to exceed six to twelve months.
    c. behavior derives from unconscious motives and drives, and problematic experiences in the unconscious mind produce dysfunction and disorders.
    d. resolution of problems is achieved by drawing out repressed information to produce greater understanding and behavioral change.

80. After identifying a specific behavior that a client wishes to change, the next priority for a social worker using a behavioral (behavior modification) approach is to:

    a. identify and evaluate the antecedents and consequences of the behavior.
    b. search for any related unconscious motivations or drives.
    c. examine the emotions associated with the target behavior.
    d. operationally define the behavior.

81. A social worker meets with a client who has significant problems with self-esteem and lacks confidence in himself and the social worker. From a psychoanalytic approach, the technique most likely to help improve the client's confidence would be:

    a. to delve into the past.
    b. sustainment.
    c. ventilation.
    d. dream analysis.

82. Using a behavioral approach (i.e., behavior modification), a social worker requires a client to keep a behavior journal. The goal of the activity is to identify all but which of the following?

    a. Behavioral frequency
    b. Behavioral intensity
    c. Behavioral patterns
    d. Behavioral resistance

83. A social worker is approached by the parents of a difficult child who tends to act out with tantrum behavior when asked to complete even simple and short chores. The social worker suggests that the parents tell the child to go ahead, scream and yell, and get it out of the way first. This technique is known as:

    a. antecedent reassignment.
    b. contracting.
    c. paradoxical direction.
    d. consequence structuring.

84. A very shy client works with an abusive, heckling, unkind coworker. The client wishes to be more assertive and defensive of himself, but his shyness prevents him from taking any self-protective action. Instead he feels anger at himself for perceived cowardice. He's taken to biting his inner lip in frustration, berating himself when alone, and his anger is fast turning inward into depression and despair. From the perspective of gestalt therapy, the client is experiencing:

    a. confluence.
    b. retroflection.
    c. projection.
    d. introjection.

85. One particular intervention technique sees a DSM-5 diagnosis as irrelevant, and is not concerned with a client's emotions, cognition, physical, psychological, or social conditions. The focus is on becoming aware of the inner and outer self, as proper awareness is all that is needed to produce change. Indeed, individuals innately possess all the necessary tools for change if their awareness regarding the need for change is adequate. This intervention perspective is called the:

    a. behavioral approach.
    b. psychoanalytic approach.
    c. cognitive approach.
    d. Gestalt approach.

86. Which key principle does NOT characterize the task-centered approach?

    a. Long-term treatment is necessary to induce change
    b. Behaviors arise from conscious choices (not by environment or learning)
    c. Individual's are fully capable to changing if they so desire
    d. A desire to change is the most crucial therapeutic factor

87. A client sees a social worker shortly after the loss of a loved one. The client relates having sent her spouse out to pick up some groceries at a nearby store. The spouse died in a car accident while returning home. The client repeats "if only I hadn't asked him to go" over and over again. According to Kübler-Ross, this client is in which stage of grief?

    a. Despair or depression
    b. Anger
    c. Bargaining
    d. Acceptance

88. A hospital emergency room social worker is asked to see a client who was treated for traumatic assault injuries following a robbery. The client is clearly fearful, vulnerable, and overwhelmed. At the time of discharge the client expresses a reluctance to leave, voicing unrealistic fears of possible further assault. The most effective intervention approach in this situation would be which of the following?

    a. Grief therapy
    b. Crisis intervention
    c. A psychoanalytic approach
    d. A task-centered approach

89. A social worker sees a newly married client who is having marital problems. The client discloses that her prior spouse was repeatedly unfaithful. She acknowledges a tendency to be overly suspicious and accusatory of her current spouse due to the persistent fears from her prior marriage. The social worker suggests that the client mentally construct a new or alternate scenario that applies to her new marriage in order to free herself from the old persistent fears. This approach would best be referred to as:

    a. complementary therapy.
    b. collaborative therapy.
    c. narrative approach.
    d. social learning approach.

90. Strategic family therapy focuses on:

    a. family communication.
    b. family structure.
    c. family rules and behavioral patterns.
    d. family subsystems.

91. A social worker sees a mother with a child recently diagnosed with juvenile onset diabetes. She is stressed and feels overwhelmed with and uncertain of the requirements of caring for this child's new special needs. This parent would best be served by joining which type of group?

    a. An educational group
    b. A support group
    c. A self-help group
    d. A task group

92. A social worker notices that the waiting area outside the pediatric intensive care unit is frequently filled with parents talking and sharing together. Over time it becomes apparent that there is an informal structure to the group, and considerable information is being exchanged (some accurate, some not). The social worker recognizes this group structure as a:

    a. formed group.
    b. natural group.
    c. closed group.
    d. structured group.

93. A social worker is working with a 42-year-old executive who is coping with a business failure and personal bankruptcy. He reveals a history of alcoholism and indicates that he is struggling with a desire to resume drinking. He resists encouragement to follow up with an Alcoholics Anonymous group. The social worker has a personal drinking history, and recognizes the warning signs. The social worker considers revealing his personal story to bolster his recommendation that the client seek help, to demonstrate understanding and empathy, and to motivate him to take further action. Which is the BEST course of action?

a. Withhold this information, because it involves personal disclosure by a social worker in a professional counseling relationship
b. Share the story, because it is entirely relevant to the client's specific situation
c. Share the story, because the consequences if the client returns to drinking are potentially severe
d. Disclose limited information, being careful not to reveal too much history, in order to motivate the client

94. Which of these efforts is NOT involved in effective group leadership?

a. Consciously using body language to facilitate communication and openness
b. Preserving an effective, safe, and nurturing group environment (ensuring quality information is shared, dispelling myths, deflecting ganging up, pairing, scapegoating, and clique [subgroup] development by some members, etc.)
c. Unconditional positive regard for and non-judgmental acceptance of group members
d. Recruiting membership to ensure a large and diverse population, ideally consisting of more than 20 group members

95. A social worker has been assigned to chair a task group. The most effective way of organizing the work of the group is by FIRST:

a. agreeing to a consensus form of decision-making.
b. specifying the group's objectives.
c. rotating the role of facilitator among group members.
d. specifying the group's objectives.

96. A social worker has been moderating a closed membership growth group and notices group members seem to be expressing more diverse opinions among themselves. This is an indication that the group has entered which stage of group development?

a. Stage 3: Intimacy
b. Stage 5: Separation
c. Stage 4: Differentiation
d. Stage 2: Power and control

97. A social worker discusses the problem of teen pregnancy at a local high school. Her supervisor wants her to design an intervention program based upon an evaluation of peer relationships, family structure, community standards, and prevailing cultural mores. The social worker had intended to intervene using a safe-sex education program obtained from a state educational service. The supervisor's approach is most likely based upon which theoretical paradigm?

a. Social learning theory
b. Cognitive theory
c. Systems theory
d. Behavioral theory

98. Following a recent remarriage a blended family has sought help from a social worker. They are struggling to develop workable family roles, standards, and cohesion. Following considerable effort, the family begins to work together better and conflicts have been largely minimized. According to eco-systems theory, the changes would best be referred to as:
   a. socialization.
   b. adaptation.
   c. role reorganization.
   d. social accommodation.

99. A couple approaches a social worker for assistance in managing conflict within their marriage. He claims she does not "fight fair" and she claims he never "hears her out." The social worker and family agree that they need to develop better communication and conflict resolution skills. The family therapy approach that best fits this couple's needs is called:
   a. the narrative approach.
   b. the structural approach.
   c. the communications approach.
   d. the social learning approach.

100. A woman seeks help for problems relating to her husband. At the outset she indicates that her husband is just like her abusive father, leading to their strained relationship. After considerable work, it becomes increasingly apparent that the husband is actually very different from her father. Instead, she has unduly focused on innocuous or irregular incidents and construed similarities within her own mind, and then projected them onto her husband. A social worker utilizing a Gestalt approach would refer to this phenomenon as:
   a. confluence.
   b. projection.
   c. introjection.
   d. retroflection.

101. The following five stage sequence addresses the key elements of a specific therapeutic modality: 1) occurrence of a significant stressor or disastrous event; 2) increased feelings of vulnerability and anxiety (as coping skills are overwhelmed); 3) a last straw event that results seeking help; 4) a period of turmoil and confusion; and 5) the mobilization of coping skills, coupled with acceptance and accommodation of change. This therapeutic modality is known as:
   a. psychoanalytic therapy.
   b. cognitive therapy.
   c. behavioral therapy.
   d. crisis intervention.

102. Following the death of a young child from cancer, a couple comes in for help in resolving complicated feelings of grief. When the couple enters the office, the social worker notes that both the husband and wife pull their chairs slightly away from each other and make no verbal, physical, or eye-contact. The social worker's best response would be to:
   a. ignore the behavior.
   b. explicitly address and explore the behavior.
   c. mention the behavior casually.
   d. confront the couple about the behavior.

103. During an initial session with a client, it becomes apparent that the client is reluctant to disclose his primary problem. Which of the following approaches would be the least effective in overcoming the client's reluctance?

 a. Developing a written contract based on specific goals and expected outcomes
 b. Simply asking the client directly why he/she is unwilling to cooperate
 c. Addressing the anticipated number of sessions, meeting frequency and duration, and the costs involved
 d. Openly acknowledging the client's reluctance to open up and share information

104. A male client tells a female social worker that he just cannot speak with a woman and requests assignment to a male social worker. The social worker's best response would be to:

 a. aid the client in exploring his difficulties in this area.
 b. explain that this should not be a problem.
 c. promptly terminate the relationship.
 d. arrange a case transfer or referral.

105. A client is seen who is in a verbally abusive relationship. She admits that he has been verbally abusive, including frequent angry outbursts, routine put-downs, and name-calling. Friends and relatives have encouraged her to end the relationship, but she continues to struggle with intense feelings of attachment and affection for him. The first step should be to:

 a. confront the client with the reality of the abuse.
 b. acknowledge the highly ambivalent feelings she is experiencing.
 c. offer reading material on abusive relationships.
 d. explore the client's other relationships, past and present.

106. A client seems to frequently have difficulty formulating her thoughts. She pauses often, partially completes her sentences, presents as somewhat helpless and needy, and seems openly eager for the social worker to do most of the talking. The most appropriate response for the social worker would be to:

 a. take over and lecture the client about her life.
 b. confront the client and demand that she talk more openly.
 c. use reflective listening techniques and allow the client more time.
 d. stop talking and use silence aggressively to stimulate discussion.

107. A social worker meets a client, and discovers that she has limited English-speaking skills. She is able to communicate her basic concerns and can respond to simple questions, but only with difficulty. At this point the social worker should do which of the following?

 a. Revise the meeting to cover only very basic issues until other arrangements can be made
 b. Delay the meeting until he/she can find an interpreter before continuing
 c. Encourage her to call a friend or family member who is more fluent and can assist her with the language barrier
 d. Terminate the meeting immediately, until he/she can arrange for her to see a social worker who speaks her native language

108. In therapeutic situations involving active or reflective listening, furthering responses (short verbal or nonverbal cues to continue) can be particularly helpful in easing the conversation along while still helping the client to feel fully heard. All of the following are examples of furthering responses EXCEPT:

a. "go on" insertions.
b. "um-hmm" or "yes" interjections.
c. "okay" declarations.
d. head nodding.

109. The physical orientation between a social worker and a client can substantially affect the communication process. Which of the following would be an optimum orientation?

a. Social worker behind a desk, client in front, clearly demonstrating authority
b. Social worker seated and client recumbent on a "therapy couch"
c. Social worker and client angled toward one another, about 90 degrees
d. Seated in two directly facing chairs

110. A question that contains multiple parts and may confuse or be unclear to a client, or make the client uncertain which part to answer first, is known as a:

a. multipart question.
b. manifold question.
c. stacked or complex question.
d. fragmented or fractured question.

111. Which is the best statement demonstrating the difference between paraphrasing and summarizing what a client has said?

a. Paraphrasing is used to correct what the client errantly said, while summarizing is used to repeat the same idea back
b. Paraphrasing is used to clarify what the client said, while summarizing is used to provide an overview of what the client said
c. Paraphrasing is used to repeat what the client has said, while summarizing is used to suggest mutual understanding
d. Paraphrasing is used to elaborate on what the client said, while summarizing is used to reiterate it

112. Reflective or active listening includes the use of nonverbal attending cues (such as making good eye contact when culturally acceptable, inclining forward attentively, using content-appropriate affective expressions, etc.), and all but which of the following?

a. Summarization ("What you're saying is...")
b. Substitution ("What I would do is...")
c. Encouragement ("Tell me more" and "Go on")
d. Clarification ("Are you saying...?").

113. When a client seems overwhelmed or uncertain how to share further, it can help to break down the concerns at hand into smaller, more manageable parts. What is this communication technique called?

a. Sequestration
b. Fragmentation
c. Downsizing
d. Partialization

114. Leading questions are often particularly problematic, as they tend to stifle communication, and normally elicit closed-ended (yes or no short-answer) responses. All of the following are examples of leading questions EXCEPT:
    a. "I think that... [decision] ...would be best, don't you?"
    b. "Could you tell me more about... [a situation] ...?"
    c. "You wouldn't want to do that, would you?"
    d. "You do know... [a certain fact] ..., don't you?"

115. Regardless of the method of communication, the recipient of information must process or interpret the information by means of:
    a. decoding.
    b. transcription.
    c. scripting.
    d. unwinding.

116. If a social worker utilizes a confrontational approach with clients, social exchange theory would suggest the most likely result would be:
    a. rapid growth on the part of the client.
    b. premature therapeutic termination by the client.
    c. increased levels of relational trust.
    d. therapeutic goal divergence.

117. According to social learning theory, one of the best ways to teach individuals better relationship skills is with:
    a. diagrammatic illustration.
    b. structured lectures.
    c. rehearsal.
    d. role play.

118. A social worker is seeing a husband and wife for marital conflict. During a session the husband reveals that he is extremely upset with the wife because she took a job outside of the home. Further exploration reveals his anger is focused on the fact that she now earns more than he does at his job of some 14 years. Which theory most likely explains his distress?
    a. Family systems theory
    b. Social role theory
    c. Cognitive theory
    d. Psychosocial theory

119. Drisko (2009) states that the five key factors necessary for a quality therapeutic relationship between client and clinician are: 1) affective attunement; 2) mutual affirmation; 3) joint efforts to resolve missteps; 4) goal congruence; and 5) _____. The fifth key factor is:
    a. the capacity to trust.
    b. accepting criticism.
    c. using varying types of empathy.
    d. the use of humor.

120. The relational concepts of preaffiliation (becoming acquainted), power and control (setting the roles), intimacy (developing cohesion), differentiation (independent opinion expression), and separation (moving to closure and termination) are all stages in:

    a. group development.
    b. team cohesion.
    c. the lifecycle of a therapeutic relationship.
    d. general relationship cycles.

121. When a social worker assesses a client's physical, social, emotional, and/or psychological needs, and specifically arranges for the ongoing provision of resources for the client, and then monitors the services involved, the social worker is acting in the role of:

    a. educator/teacher.
    b. broker.
    c. advocate.
    d. case manager.

122. A social worker sees clients through a court-ordered treatment program. In treating reluctant involuntary clients, the MOST difficult issue is:

    a. the limited availability of help for the client.
    b. client anger at being coerced into the treatment process.
    c. client ambivalence about the need for treatment.
    d. the social worker's own personal feelings about the kind of problem being treated.

123. Louise began therapy with a presenting problem of experiencing increasing anxiety and panic attacks when driving alone or riding in the car with her husband. As the social worker took her history, she also learned that Louise has been having marital problems and is considering leaving her husband, but is terrified of being alone again. When Louise casually mentions that she doesn't feel anxious when riding with her friends as a passenger, her social worker intuits that the marriage trouble and the driving phobia are related, and that the client's panic is arising from her feelings about her marriage. Which type of content has brought the therapist to this hypothesis about her client's presenting problem?

    a. Neurotic symptoms
    b. Overt content
    c. Manifest content
    d. Latent content

124. Upon first meeting a client, a social worker should begin by taking which of the following steps (in the order listed)?

    a. Assess the client, summarize legal and ethical obligations, complete a service contract, and establish a rapport
    b. Establish rapport, summarize legal and ethical obligations, complete a service contract, and assess the client
    c. Complete a service contract and summarize legal and ethical obligations
    d. Summarize legal and ethical obligations, complete a counseling contract, explore the client's presenting problem, and assess the client

125. Specific treatment approaches, such as the communications approach (which sees communication deficits as central to interpersonal dysfunction), the structural approach (which views interpersonal interactions as central to dysfunction), the social learning approach (focusing on improving interactive skills such as conflict resolution and communication), and the narrative approach (using personal stories, ideas, thoughts, and revisions, to discover and implement new behavior patterns) are associated with:

a. behavioral therapy.
b. cognitive therapy.
c. group therapy.
d. family therapy.

126. A social worker has a genuine attraction for a client. While the client has shown no romantic interest in him, and he feels he has maintained proper boundaries, he notices that he is thinking of her more and more often outside of the therapeutic context. The best way for the social worker to resolve this issue would be to:

a. disclose his feelings to the client, so that they can both monitor boundaries.
b. terminate the client immediately, and refer the client elsewhere.
c. seek supervisory or other consultation to explore the situation further.
d. take no action, as nothing untoward is occurring.

127. In referring clients to appropriate organizational and community resources, a social worker is serving primarily serving in the role of:

a. advocate.
b. broker.
c. educator/teacher.
d. lobbyist.

128. A social worker sees two clients through a corporate agency. A husband, experiencing significant marital discord, seeks counseling services. After a few sessions, it becomes clear that the wife has traits of a serious mental health disorder, and over time she is seen exclusively. Two months have passed since the last contact with the husband. The primary client is:

a. the couple.
b. the wife.
c. the corporation/agency.
d. the husband.

129. The National Association of Social Workers (NASW) defines the mission of social work as including all of the following EXCEPT:

a. meeting the needs of individuals in a family and social context.
b. building the profession to be superior to other social interventionists.
c. promoting human well-being and aiding others to secure basic human needs.
d. addressing problems from a societal and environmental perspective.

130. The core values of social work include all of the following EXCEPT:

a. competence; dignity of the individual.
b. integrity; importance of human relationships.
c. acclimation; accommodation.
d. service; social justice.

131. The ethical responsibility to disclose to a client all the associated costs, risks, and benefits of a proposed treatment, and then to obtain the client's explicit agreement before embarking on the proposed treatment, is known as:

 a. informed consent.
 b. therapeutic contracting.
 c. setting goals and objectives.
 d. affirmative assent.

132. A social worker can freely breech client confidentiality without informed consent in which of the following situation(s)?

 a. Upon receipt of a subpoena
 b. When contacted by law enforcement
 c. In situations of suspected child abuse
 d. All of the above

133. Barbara has learned that her new client, Jim, is also her mother's legal advisor, and he occasionally lunches with her mother to discuss business. Her mother is unaware of the counseling relationship between them. Barbara explains to Jim that there is a conflict of interest in their working together and that her main concern is making sure his interests and confidentiality remain protected. What is the BEST action Barbara can take next?

 a. Keep working with Jim, but try to be aware of potential conflicts
 b. Refer Jim to someone else
 c. Ask Jim to tell her mother about the counseling arrangement
 d. Terminate the counseling relationship

134. The Federal Privacy Act of 1974 (i.e., PL 93-579) requires that clients be informed: 1) when records about them are being maintained; 2) that they have a right to access these records; 3) that they have a right to copies (provided they bear the costs); and 4) that the records will only be used for the purpose they were created unless they provide written release or consent otherwise. Exceptions include: 1) sharing with agency employees on a "need-to-know" basis; 2) legitimate research, if identifying information is removed; and all but one of the following:

 a. responding to an emergency to protect another individual.
 b. publication in a reputable professional journal.
 c. responding to a court order or subpoena.
 d. providing information to government agencies for legitimate law-enforcement purposes.

135. Malpractice liability generally runs from an agency's board of directors, to the director, supervisory staff, and then to the front-line social worker. Employer and supervisor liability accrue under the legal theory of:

 a. proxy liability.
 b. substitute liability.
 c. hierarchical liability.
 d. vicarious liability.

136. An oncology social worker has been seeing a 16-year-old via a medical clinic. He has a cerebral glioma (brain tumor). A year ago the tumor was surgically resected. Since that time, however, the tumor has returned and infiltrated surrounding brain tissue. It cannot be removed. Repeated surgeries and chemotherapy have been tried, but the condition is terminal. A further tumor "debulking" surgery has been scheduled with the parents' approval. However, the teen does not want further treatment. The initial social work response should be which of the following?

   a. Refer the case to a bioethics committee
   b. Explore both treatment and non-treatment views and options
   c. Advocate for the teen, as he must experience the burdens
   d. Advocate for the parents' desires as legal decision-makers

137. A 34-year-old male is being seen in a court-ordered anger management program. He has a history of assaultive behavior with multiple arrests in the past. Most recently, he was arrested for assaulting his live-in girlfriend with whom he shares a child. This arrest resulted in the current counseling. The girlfriend has allowed a restraining order to lapse, and has permitted him back in the home. During a session, the client becomes agitated and angry when discussing the girlfriend's "controlling ways." He abruptly terminates the session by stalking out saying he will have to "deal with her" himself. No explicit threat was voiced, but his level of anger was high and his history is concerning. The proper social work response would be:

   a. to call law enforcement for a consultation.
   b. to carefully document the session and concerns to protect oneself from possible subsequent liability.
   c. to call the girlfriend and let her know of the concerns, given his level of agitation when he left the office.
   d. to do nothing, as no explicit threat was made.

138. A woman who has been diagnosed with HIV/AIDS is being seen in a public health clinic. She has revealed that she is having unprotected sex with a new boyfriend. Further, she shares needles with him in mutual drug use situations. She states that he does not know she has AIDS. She has been counseled at length to reveal her HIV/AIDS status to the boyfriend, but she refuses to comply. She states that he will leave her if she reveals this, and she flatly refuses to disclose her condition to him. Which would be the most appropriate social work response?

   a. Tell the client that if she does not discontinue the behaviors or have the boyfriend inform the social worker that he is aware, the social worker will be required to warn him over her objections
   b. Call local law enforcement and ask them to evaluate the situation
   c. Continue counseling her, but do not explicitly address the situation further
   d. Make an immediate effort to contact the boyfriend and warn him

139. The two most commonly overlooked trauma issues in returning military veterans are:

   a. lengthy tours of duty and traumatic brain injury.
   b. traumatic brain injury and sexual assault trauma.
   c. survivor's guilt and lengthy tours of duty.
   d. sexual assault trauma and lengthy tours of duty.

140. Federal protection for personal health records privacy was enacted in 1996. The legislation applies to all health care providers, health care clearinghouses, and health plan providers. It sets limits on the disclosure and uses of patient records. It also provides for individual access to medical records, and it establishes the right to receive notices of privacy practices. This legislation is known as:

a. The Health Insurance Portability and Accountability Act of 1996 (HIPAA).
b. The Health Insurance Portability and Accountability Act of 1996 (HIPAA).
c. The Health Records Privacy and Accountability Act of 1996 (HRPAA).
d. The Health Records Privacy Act of 1996 (HRPA).

141. While numerous laws and policies address the confidentiality of medical, counseling, and other health care discussions and records, certain exceptions to confidentiality do exist. These include: 1) mandated reporting issues; 2) subpoenas or other court orders; 3) treatment continuity (cross-coverage by other agency staff); and all of the following EXCEPT:

a. disclosures regarding abuse of a child (e.g., mandated reporting, violations of the law, etc.).
b. disclosures to an employer providing insurance coverage.
c. disclosures released at a client's written request.
d. disclosures for insurance coverage purposes.

142. Before a social worker can release any information from discussions with a client or from a client's case records, which of the following must be met?

a. The client must agree that information can be released
b. The client must sign a paper that information can be released
c. Informed consent criteria for information release must be met
d. All of the above

143. The brother of an agency secretary has offered to help out at an agency retreat. He is managing refreshments and coordinating the event with owners of the hosting physical facility. During the course of the retreat, the brother overhears the name of a public figure who is receiving counseling via the agency. The brother's obligation(s) and legal liability as related to confidentiality can best be described as which of the following?

a. He has no obligation or legal liability
b. As a volunteer at the activity he has legal liability
c. He has a moral obligation but no legal liability
d. He is both ethically and legally liable

144. A client with a serious personality disorder and a history of violence demands copies of his counseling records. He is willing and able to pay for the copies he is requesting. Extremely sensitive information is in the case record. The social worker's obligation in releasing the records to the client can best be described as which of the following?

a. Laws, ethics, and policy will require the information to be released
b. A case summary can be released, but no actual copies need be provided
c. Records may be withheld based upon issues of a possible adverse reaction
d. The agency may impose exorbitant copy costs to discourage release

145. The basic functions of administrators include: 1) monitoring, reviewing, advising, and evaluating employees; 2) planning and delegation; and all but which one of the following?

a. Planning and delegation
b. Conflict resolution and mediation
c. Advocacy (both horizontally with departmental staff, and vertically between other departments and staff)
d. Frontline organizational services

146. A supervisor's role involves: 1) being a role model; 2) recruitment and orientation; 3) day-to-day management; 4) staff training, education, and development; 5) staff assessments and reviews; and all but which one of the following?

a. Providing support and counsel to staff
b. Evaluating the program for ongoing improvement
c. Allocating interdepartmental operating funds
d. Advocating for staff and program needs

147. The following are all comparisons between consultation and supervision EXCEPT:

a. consultation is episodic (as sought) and voluntary, while supervision is ongoing and mandatory.
b. consultants provide advice and recommendations, while supervisors tend to provide binding directives and procedures.
c. consultants may have broad administrative authority, while supervisors have only interdepartmental authority.
d. consultation is provided by an outside expert, while supervision is provided by an internal staff leader.

148. A supervisor may approach a staff supervision experience from the perspective of specific traits and characteristics that appear to influence the practice situation. This approach is referred to as the:

a. interactional perspective
b. situational perspective
c. personality perspective
d. organizational perspective

149. At what minimum frequency should supervisors provide staff meetings and/or individual staff supervision?

a. Daily
b. Monthly
c. Weekly
d. Quarterly

150. It is the responsibility of a supervisor to ensure that all staff members are well-trained and effective at their jobs. This can be accomplished by way of direct instruction, in-house staff training programs, workshops, and continuing education courses. The most effective educational approach is to employ:

a. case reviews.
b. role playing.
c. observation.
d. records reviews.

151. A supervisor is approached by a staff person with multiple personal and family issues. At some point it becomes evident that the staff person needs to receive professional counseling to resolve deep-seated issues that affect job performance as well as other intimate relationships. The best role for a supervisor in this situation is to do which of the following?

- a. Provide offsite private counseling in addition to staff supervision
- b. Provide informal counseling and staff supervision onsite
- c. Urge the staff member to obtain professional counseling elsewhere
- d. Refrain from making any suggestions regarding personal issues

152. What is the difference between statistical reliability and validity?

- a. Reliability indicates whether or not a test measures the proposed data well; validity refers to the level of statistical significance
- b. Reliability addresses whether or not the test results are correct; validity examines whether or not they are verifiable
- c. Reliability requires consistent results over multiple test administrations; validity refers to whether or not the test actually measures what it claims to measure
- d. Reliability is a measure of test process; validity is a measure of test outcome

153. A social worker has been asked to evaluate client satisfaction by age. Thus, the social worker assigns all individuals receiving counseling services at the clinic into decade-based age groups, and then randomly selects individuals from each age group for a short satisfaction survey. This overall sampling approach is known as:

- a. stratified random sampling.
- b. cluster sampling.
- c. systematic sampling.
- d. simple random sampling.

154. An emergency room social worker is called to assist a young male adult with acute appendicitis. The appendix has not yet ruptured, but if it does the condition will be life-threatening. For non-emergent surgeries, administration dictates that patients produce proof of insurance or pay upfront. For life-threatening conditions, the law requires treatment. The student is a black male from Africa and is legally in the country on a student visa. If the student was illegally in the country, the surgery would be provided under current state law, but as he entered on a valid visa, state assistance is not available. The medical staff is frustrated, as they do not want the condition to progress, endangering the patient and resulting in a more complex surgery. Which of the following would not be a proper response?

- a. Pursue possible Hill-Burton (Title XVI) funding in his behalf
- b. Request a re-evaluation and reconsideration of the patient's condition in light of EMTALA regulations
- c. Pursue funding via his country's embassy
- d. Tell medical staff that no help is available

155. The term deinstitutionalization refers to which of the definitions below?

a. A philosophy of client- social worker collaboration in treatment, as opposed to hierarchical social worker-driven treatment
b. Changes in policy and law that led to the release of many disabled patients who would have otherwise remained in institutional settings
c. Creating a treatment program that serves the needs of the client, as opposed to the needs of the institution
d. Helping a client accommodate to a community living environment after having been institutionalized for an extended period (usually, years)

156. A 48-year-old construction worker fell from a scaffold and was left permanently disabled due to brain injury when he struck his head upon landing. The hospital social worker should ensure that application is first made for:

a. social security disability.
b. supplemental security income.
c. Medicaid.
d. worker's compensation.

157. The original Social Security Act was passed in 1935. It was a federal trust fund that was intended to primarily provide "old age and survivors" benefits. To be eligible for full benefits, an individual born before 1960 must have attained the age of:

a. 55.
b. 62.
c. 65.
d. 67.

158. The federal health insurance program for the elderly is known as Medicare, and was designed for individuals over the age of 65, or the disabled, or individuals with end-stage renal disease (ESRD). Originally, this insurance had two specific components. Which are they?

a. Hospital insurance and drug coverage
b. Medical insurance and drug coverage
c. Physician insurance and hospital insurance
d. Medical insurance and hospital insurance

159. The Elderly Nutrition Program, Food Stamps, School Lunch Program, and Women, Infants and Children (WIC) program are:

a. funded by the state and locally administered.
b. funded by the state and federally administered.
c. funded federally and locally administered.
d. funded federally and state administered.

160. Government sponsored social service policies can be categorized into all of the following groups EXCEPT:

a. demographic programs.
b. exceptional eligibility programs.
c. selective eligibility programs.
d. universal programs.

161. A client who has qualified for and been awarded Medicaid benefits is having difficulty finding a dentist willing to provide dental services for the Medicaid reimbursement rates. A local community organization has offered to voluntarily augment the Medicaid payment rate to ensure the dental care will be provided promptly. Federal guidelines mandate that:

    a. the patient be billed no more than 20% of the rate.
    b. the health provider must accept Medicaid as payment in full.
    c. only usual and customary fees be charged beyond Medicaid.
    d. the patient opt out of Medicaid if another payment source is available.

162. Prior to 1996, the TANF program (Temporary Assistance for Needy Families) was known as:

    a. General Assistance.
    b. Aid for Families with Dependent Children.
    c. Government-Sponsored Welfare.
    d. Indigent Adult and Family Assistance.

163. The key benefits of bureaucratic organization are the efficient allocation of resources and the specialized skills developed by various bureaucratic employees. The key deficiency inherent in a bureaucratic structure is:

    a. the recruitment of staff based primarily on technical and professional qualifications.
    b. the division of labor according to specialization and tasks.
    c. the universal application of rigid rules and procedures.
    d. the rational organization of services around specific goals.

164. All of the following are basic administrative functions EXCEPT:

    a. planning and delegation.
    b. conflict resolution and mediation.
    c. employee monitoring, reviews, and advocacy.
    d. providing front-line services to agency clients.

165. The key features and/or benefits of a not-for-profit (non-profit) organization, as compared with a for-profit organization include:

    a. an orientation toward non-commercial goods and services as opposed to selling products and services.
    b. organizational members obtain no benefits via investment or shareholding in the organization.
    c. greater control over assets and revenue.
    d. differing classification by the IRS for purposes of revenue taxation.

166. The term operating revenue refers to:

    a. the funds derived through the provision of services and/ or goods.
    b. the gains or losses resulting from normal business operations.
    c. the bottom line of the organization's financial operations.
    d. the net assets of a business at the time of an audit.

167. The SOAP method of progress notation is commonly used in which of the following forms of recording-keeping?

a. Narrative Recording
b. Person-Oriented Recording
c. Problem-Oriented Recording
d. Process Recording

168. The most rigorous form of program outcome evaluation is:

a. the decision-oriented approach.
b. an experimental evaluation.
c. a customer and peer review.
d. a performance audit.

169. A social worker has been asked to evaluate program effectiveness at multiple community senior day care centers. The most effective approach to take would be:

a. action research.
b. self-evaluation.
c. point-specific research.
d. cluster evaluation.

170. Which of the following is not a key difference between agency administration and agency staff supervision?

a. Administrators are focused on service quality, while supervisors are focused on staff competence
b. Administrators focus externally (i.e., on the community and other issues outside the agency), while supervisors focus internally
c. Administrators are responsible for program development, while supervisors are focused on program implementation
d. Administrators are charged with overall agency funding, while supervisors are charged with successful budgeting

Answer Key and Explanations for Test #2

1. B: The fundamental premise of Freud's psychoanalytic theory is that human behavior is best understood as arising from drives and unconscious motivations. An individual may also respond to environmental stimuli, such as peer pressure, and the need for power and control. However, self-initiated behaviors are frequently the result of unconscious motivations, drives, and desires. Behaviors are shaped by repressed experiences and memories from childhood, and will reflect a related covert purpose. According to Freud, there are three levels of consciousness: the unconscious mind (containing thoughts and ideas that are hidden from awareness), the preconscious mind (containing thoughts beyond active awareness, but which can easily be accessed and recognized), and the conscious mind (containing thoughts and motivations which are already in full awareness, and thus can readily be manipulated, accessed, and otherwise utilized).

2. D: Repression is the process through which distressing and anxiety-provoking thoughts may be rejected by the conscious mind and forced into the unconscious mind.

3. C: According to Freud, mental disturbances and psychological maladjustments are primarily the result of conflicts between the id, ego, and superego. These three elements of an individual's personality must be unified and work together smoothly for optimum mental health. Only through adequate coordination of these elements can an individual successfully meet fundamental desires and needs without generating psychological dissonance and conflict. When any of these basic elements of the personality are in conflict, an individual will be hampered in securing basic needs and desires, and frustration will result. The extent of psychiatric maladjustment is a function of the degree of disharmony between these three personality elements.

4. C: Burnout is characterized by feeling that one has more responsibility than control. (Note that there is no change in Maria's outward behavior: She is not in crisis and is not presenting with symptoms of unusual anxiety).

5. A: According to Freud, personality development is accomplished through a series of psychosexual stages that culminate before the onset of latency (age 6 to puberty). This process is completed by 5 years of age. Freud's primary focus on an individual's past arose from his theory of personality development. He postulated that patterns of adult behavior reflect the blueprint created during the earliest years of life, as childhood solutions to problems continue to manifest. Thus, Freud postulated that two major aspects shape personality development: 1) natural growth and maturation through five stages of psychosexual development; and 2) the degree of success an individual experiences in overcoming anxieties, conflicts, and frustrations, and in avoiding pain.

6. D: These terms refer to driving forces. The term cathexis refers to the urging force that individuals experience to pursue the unconscious wishes and desires of the id. The term anti-cathexis refers to the checking force that enables individuals to resist the urges of the id. Collectively these forces are referred to as driving forces. An individual's ultimate mental state emerges as a function of the processes of exchange between the driving forces.

7. B: The more clearly that goals are defined, the more likely they are to be attained. Likewise, clear-cut agreements about timetables, payment, rights, and responsibilities set the stage for a transparent therapeutic alliance.

8. C: The phallic stage typically occurs during 3-6 years of age. In ascending age order, the stages include:

- The oral stage: (0-18 months of age) Characterized by a focus on oral pleasure (sucking, eating, oral exploration of items, etc.).
- The anal stage: (18 months to 3 years of age) Characterized by a focus on the anal experience of elimination and resolved once sphincter control is mastered.
- The phallic stage: (3-6 years of age) Characterized by a focus on the genitals.
- The latency stage: (6-12 years of age) Characterized by the onset of sexuality within socially acceptable bounds, and terminating at the onset of puberty.
- The genital stage: (12 years of age and above) Characterized by genitalia acceptance, and mature sexual feelings.

9. D: It was Anna Freud who proposed the idea that significant threats to the ego could provoke powerful symptoms of anxiety, which served to stimulate the deployment any of a variety of psychological defense mechanisms. These defense mechanisms constitute irrational and unconscious efforts to protect the ego from anxiety and distress by means of reality distortion, denial, or avoidance. Defense mechanisms often serve a vital role, allowing the unconscious mind time to accommodate and prepare for a difficult psychic insult (i.e., denial at a time of unexpected loss, etc.). If taken to an extreme and perpetuated, however, psychological pathology may develop and require intervention.

10. B: Reaction formation is the act of substituting an opposite response to relieve distress. Each of the above descriptions addresses partial aspects of the defense mechanism known as reaction formation. However, B is the best and most complete description. Reaction formation occurs when an opposing response to the one internally felt is substituted in order to relieve internal dissonance or distress. Specific examples include: 1) someone "bending over backwards" to favor a coworker to cover an intense dislike of the individual, 2) an individual undertaking a public campaign against a vice that he secretly practices, and 3) a married woman treating a man rudely to compensate for the distress of internally feeling attracted to him.

11. A: Splitting is the action of suppressing the contradictory qualities of a given entity or situation. The primary feature of splitting is the defining and separation of good and bad in order to maintain psychic well-being. For example, describing a boss who fired you as "all bad" to avoid the guilt of deserved dismissal. This defense mechanism can lead to psychopathology when it is encountered in highly important relationships early in the developmental process. As a primitive defense mechanism, it may be engaged in infancy and thus shape later life. For example, in coping with a mother who alternates between nurturance and abuse, a child may vacillate between feelings of safety and danger, and be unable to reconcile the two in ego development. This may result in a "fragmented self" that handicaps meaningful relationships—where fundamental trust cannot be established and vacillating definitions of good and bad are arbitrarily imposed.

12. C: These terms are aspects of adaptation. Ego psychology emphasizes the ego structure of the personality, and the behavioral patterns and perceptions by which individuals adapt to their social environment. Adaptation, and the skills and abilities to accomplish it, is the primary focus. Ego psychology postulates that adaptation is a process of mutual exchange between an individual and the surrounding environment. Alloplastic behavior refers to situations where the social environment itself is altered to facilitate adaptation. Autoplastic behavior refers to individual changes in behavior to facilitate adaptation in a social environment. According to ego psychology, human behavior primarily arises from efforts of environmental adaptation.

13. D: Hartmann, unlike Freud, believed that children are born with both ids and egos. Therefore, Hartmann felt that children have the rudimentary capacity to begin rationally considering the need for mediation demands between themselves and their environment. Option A is not correct because it was Freud that placed the greatest emphasis on the past over current social environments. Option B refers to a concept espoused by both Freud and Hartmann. Option C is incorrect because both theorists saw defense mechanisms as strategies related to the ego and not the id.

14. B: Idealization and intellectualization are not part of the first six ego functions. The concepts of idealization and intellectualization refer to defense mechanisms, as proposed by Anna Freud. Judgment refers to recognition and evaluation of consequences prior to taking action. Regulation and control over drives and impulses refers to the capacity to control necessary impulses and to conform behavior to reality. Reality testing refers to the capacity to perceive the self and the external environment. Sense of reality refers to the capacity for accurate perception of things and experiences. Thought processes refers to the capacity to be realistic, organized, and goal-oriented. Object relations refers to the capacity to interact meaningfully with others.

15. D: Displacement and substitution are not part of the second group of six ego functions. The concepts of displacement and substitution refer to defense mechanisms, as proposed by Anna Freud. Autonomous functions are functions independent of psychic conflict that operate continuously (e.g., memory, concentration, perception, etc.). Integrative functioning refers to the capacity for parts of the personality to integrate in order to resolve conflicts. Stimulus barrier refers to functions that remain stable despite elevations or reductions in stimulation. Mastery-competence refers to the capacity of an individual to engage and interact successfully with their environment. Defensive functioning refers to the capacity to maintain functioning by drawing upon unconscious mechanisms needed to moderate painful experiences and anxiety.

16. A: The influential Swiss thinker Carl Jung is known as the founder of analytical psychology. He played no key role in the development of object relations theory. Object relations theory was derived from Freudian psychoanalytic theory and ego psychology. key concepts of object relations theory include: 1) Mahler's view that object relations emerge during ego organization as a child learns to differentiate self from others during the first three and a half years of life. 2) Object relations are developed because individuals are driven to build interpersonal relationships from birth forward, which necessitates a sense of self and others. 3) All interpersonal relationships are affected by the sense of self and others ultimately obtained by the individual.

17. A: The symbiotic stage of development occurs from 1 to 5 months after birth. The autistic stage encompasses the first month and is characterized by total self-absorption and a lack of response to external stimuli. During the symbiotic stage, the child becomes aware of the need-satisfying object (mother) as a separate being. The separation-individuation stage occurs between 5 months and 24 months of age, and has four substages:

1. Differentiation (5-9 months): Attention shifts outward and early caregiver separations occur (crawling away, etc.).
2. Practicing (9-14 months): Autonomous ego functions emerge as mobility increases.
3. Rapprochement (14-24 months): Desires for independence increase, but frequent checks ensure the caregiver remains present.
4. Object constancy (after 24 months): The caregiver is internalized, and there is an understanding the caregiver exists despite any absence.

18. D: The self/self-object relationship is the key difference between self-psychology and object relations theory. In object relations theory, certain objects provide essential affirmation of the self at key developmental points (principally, the mother or other important caregiver, who provides necessary attention, nurturance, and praise to engender a sense of value and self-worth). Then, in the process of ego development, the self separates and individuates from the object, and an independent sense of self emerges. In self-psychology, however, the importance of key objects (called self-objects) persists. While the self-objects from which intrapsychic support is derived may change and evolve (from parents to spouse, from educational attainment to careers, etc.), the role remains central to psychological well-being and optimum functioning (i.e., total separation and individuation does not occur). The persistent bonds between the self and important self-objects is illustrated by the term self/self-object.

19. C: Empathetic mirroring is the empathic process by which the self-object fully accepts the embryonic grandiose self. The infant's immature ego tends to construct an embryonic "grandiose" image of the self. This positive self-image is affirmed and sustained by the empathic support and nurturance of the primary self-object (typically the mother). Further validation comes from, as Kohut puts it, "the radiance of the mother's eyes" when regarding her offspring. The aggregate result is referred to as empathic mirroring, which engenders idealized affirmation of the self and deep nurturance and bonding.

20. B: Transmuting internalization is the process by which the grandiose self internalizes (or "transmutes") ideals, goals, and values from the self-object (most prominently from the mother, as nurturer, and father as protector—each, what Kohut called an idealized "parent imago") into a cohesive self-structure. The transmuting process gradually includes integration of the functions performed by the self-object for the child's self, making the internalization process of all self-object features complete. The process of transmuting internalization is ineffective if empathic mirroring has failed, leading to two forms of narcissism—involving both the self and the self-object—and preventing the construction of a cohesive and healthy self.

21. A: Gestalt theory and Freud's psychoanalytic theory agree that issues and problems are integral to personal experiences. Both gestalt theory and psychoanalytic theory recognize the influence of past experiences and the environment in shaping current behavior. However, gestalt theory primarily focuses on the present, while psychoanalytic theory is intensely focused on the past. Gestalt theory also differs from psychoanalytic theory in that personality structure is seen as largely integrated (as opposed to interrelated) but distinctly separate systems. Finally, gestalt theory sees each individual from a holistic, total-person perspective (indeed, the word gestalt is derived from a German word for wholeness), as opposed to evaluating fragments of the self.

22. C: Lifespan development theories attempt to explain human development and behavior through the entire lifecycle. Among the earliest theorists attempting to construct such a theoretical model was Erik Erikson. He developed the psychosocial theory of human behavior and personality, which addresses psychosocial stages of development from birth to senior years. Erikson's eight stages of psychosocial development build on each other, incorporate specific developmental ego crises, and embody various conflicts that must be resolved for successful personal progress to be achieved. The conflicts involve polarizing personality features referred to as dystonic and syntonic traits that must be balanced for healthy development, though ideally tending toward syntonic aspects.

23. D: Successful personality development requires individuals to cope with negative (dystonic) threats to self-integrity, and to integrate positive (syntonic) personality skills. Personality development involves engaging increasingly complex and/or burdensome challenges, and successfully overcoming each in order to master each maturational stage. Erikson refers to the engagement process as a psychosocial crisis, and views each stage as having been optimally mastered when the outcome tends toward a syntonic-biased balance.

24. B: During this stage (Stage 2) between 2-3 years of age, children acquire the verbal and motor skills that facilitate autonomy. The positive result is an increased sense of autonomy and self-mastery, while children denied adequate nurturance and social opportunities tend toward self-doubt, shame, and insecurity. The first developmental stage (Stage 1: birth to 1 year) addresses the emergence of trust versus mistrust, which is primarily a function of receiving adequate nurturance and love. Stage 3 (4-5 years of age) addresses initiative versus guilt, which requires adequate self-initiative opportunities through safe exploration and shared play experiences. Stage 4 (6-11 years of age) involves industry versus inferiority and emerges from personal task accomplishment and learning, which, if inadequate, results in feelings of incompetence and inferiority.

25. A: Sophie is focusing on her client's strengths using a strengths-based perspective, which has been shown to empower clients and build resiliency. Solution-focused perspectives focus on end goals and methods to reach those goals. A structural perspective focuses on identifying the interacting elements of the client system and which areas require attention to regain stabilization. A behavioral perspective would focus on behaviors that contribute to and surround the client's gambling addiction and finding ways to control or discourage those behaviors.

26. C: These skills are developed between 15-17 months of age. In the first thirty days of life, newborn development is focused on sensory functions (vision, oral stimulation, etc.) and primary reflexes (sucking, grasping, etc.). At one month, arm and leg reflexes emerge and overall strength increases. The second month of life includes reaching for objects, holding the head up, hair growth, etc. During the third month, strength increases to elevate the chest when lying on the stomach. The fourth month encompasses teething and head turning. In the fifth month, eye-hand coordination improves, and locomotion by rocking and rolling is pursued. From 6-8 months, the focus is on crawling, sitting up with help, and balance improvements. At 9-12 months locomotion expands to include walking, standing alone, and finally climbing stairs or steps with help. Between 15-17 months independent walking, throwing, and eventually walking sideways and backwards will typically be learned.

27. A: Differences in motor skills between males and females are most evident between 7-11 years of age. At 18-19 months of age, toddlers can speak words and short phrases, jump with both feet and run, and grasp and release. At 2 years bladder control emerges, vocabulary grows (at least 50 words), and at least two words can be joined into a sentence. At 3-4 years the child dresses, draws circles, and scribbles. By age 6, name printing, early reading, and permanent teeth are noted. From ages 7-11, girls' fine-motor skills advance more than boys. Between 12-15 years of age coordination improves and pubescence begins. At 16-18 years of age, sexual maturity occurs, muscle growth increases, and height growth slows. From 18-30 years of age, body fat increases and height diminishes. Between 35-60 years of age, senses and motor skills diminish, and females enter menopause. From 60-70 years, decreases in senses continue, as does hair and tooth loss and overall height. From the age of 70 and onward, physical deterioration becomes more rapid.

28. B: Schemas refer to goal-oriented strategies for learning. Piaget offers a theory focused on cognitive development. The theory explores how individuals learn by organizing their thoughts and knowledge as they explore their environment. Learning takes place by adaptation, which consists of assimilation (adding new information to existing understandings) and accommodation (modifying thinking and knowledge to meet environmental and new object demands). Piaget proposed four stages of cognitive development in children: sensorimotor, pre-operational, concrete operational, and formal operational.

29. B: A child begins to use symbols during the pre-operational stage. The sensorimotor stage extends from birth to about 2 years of age. During this period the senses and motor functions are used to interact with the world. Stimulus-response circular reactions are noted (i.e., thumb-sucking feels good, so more thumb-sucking is pursued). Symbolic understandings are not possible, so people or things are "gone" if they are not fully evident. The pre-operational stage (2-7 years of age) is characterized by the use of symbols (images, drawings, words, etc.), language (speech), conceptualization of a past and future (i.e., promise something "soon" and the child will understand), and egocentricity (everything is seen as relative to him/herself).

30. A: The concrete operational stage extends from 7-11 years of age, and is characterized by an awareness that any single item or substance, divided into smaller parts, is still the same quantity as that of the undivided original whole (called conservation of substance); and the capacity for logical manipulation of symbols (i.e., re-organizing things changes only the order, not the things themselves). The formal operational stage (11-15 years of age) is characterized by adult-like thinking, including abstract thinking (also known as hypothetical thinking).

31. C: Alfred Adler and Albert Ellis are the two most prominent cognitive theorist from the group listed. Cognitive theorists posit that thoughts and other cognitions are the primary motivators of behavior, although environment and physical factors may have some collateral influence. Cognition is also seen as the source of emotions. Unconscious beliefs, along with chemical, neurological, and other physiological disturbances play a significant role in human behavior, but conscious thought can play a more determinative role. Although Adler began his career with Sigmund Freud, cognitive theory departs from Freudian theory in three key ways: 1) the personality is a holistic entity, and not a component system (i.e., not separated into id, ego, and superego components); 2) social motivation, rather than sexual drive, shapes most behavior; and 3) conscious thoughts and beliefs are far more significant than unconscious motivations.

32. D: Another name for rational emotive therapy is the ABC Theory of Emotion. Rational emotive therapy was developed by Albert Ellis, and is based on a cognitive-behavioral theory. The theory posits that an activating event induces beliefs and thoughts, which result in emotional and behavioral consequences. Per Ellis, rational thoughts in response to any event or environmental context will result in healthy and functional behavioral consequences. Conversely, irrational thoughts result in dysfunctional disturbed behavior. Therefore, the therapeutic goal is to assist individuals to develop rational and functional responses to environmental and situational challenges.

33. B: Kohlberg's theory was an extension of Jean Piaget's theory of cognitive development. Kohlberg was impressed with Piaget's conception of personality development in stages. However, he believed that moral development involved a more protracted and complicated developmental process than Piaget had postulated. Kohlberg felt that morals (ethics, honesty, altruism, etc.) were absent in the newborn, and that age was less a predictor of moral development than was intelligence and social interaction. Thus, innate cognitive ability and social experiences (especially via the family) were the primary source of moral development.

34. A: Kohlberg proposed three levels with two stages in each level in his stages of moral development. The pre-conventional level typically unfolds between birth and age 9, with more progress at later ages. Stage 1 most often is encountered at school age, and is characterized by obedience and a desire to avoid punishment. Stage 2, is characterized by a personal gain (best interests) orientation. The conventional level, usually unfolds between the ages of 9 to 15. Stage 3 involves acting to gain the approval (and avoid the disapproval) of others. Stage 4 involves an awareness to conform to proper laws and rules. The post-conventional level is normally engaged between age 15 and adulthood. Stage 5 is characterized by the concept of social contracts and genuine interest and mutuality. Stage 6 is the pinnacle of moral development, and involves a universal ethical view and autonomous morality based entirely on conscious. Kohlberg suggested that few, if any, ever reach this stage.

35. B: An example of negative reinforcement is the removal of an adverse stimulus following a positive behavior. Punishment involves the application of a negative stimulus for negative behavior. Negative reinforcement, however, involves the removal of a negative stimulus in response to positive behavior (i.e., nagging stops when a desired behavior occurs). Positive reinforcement involves the application of a reward (praise, any object, approval, etc.) for engaging in a specific positive behavior. The concepts of reinforcement and punishment are key elements in operant conditioning theory, as provided by the behavioral theorist, B.F. Skinner.

36. C: Classical conditioning theory is also known as respondent conditioning theory. The classical conditioning theory was formulated by John Watson and Ivan Pavlov. This theory suggests that all behaviors can be changed, because all behaviors are learned. Behaviors stem from identifiable stimuli, with either a voluntary (emitted) or involuntary (reflexive) response resulting. By taking an unconditioned stimulus (US), and linking it with its unconditioned response (UR), a specific stimulus (conditioned stimulus) can be introduced that will, if reinforced, produced an eventual conditioned response. For example, hunger (an environmental condition), coupled with food (US), will lead to salivation (UR). If food and a specific signal (US) are presented together often enough (conditioning), eventually the signal alone (CS) will induce salivation (CR).

37. D: An antecedent event is best described as an external event occurring immediately prior to a specific behavior. Social Learning Theory posits that behavioral change can be achieved by manipulating either the antecedents or consequences associated with a specific behavior. Therefore, all behaviors are learned and can be changed. First a specific behavior is identified. Then all relevant antecedent events and consequences of the behavior are identified. Finally, changes are made in the most influential and malleable antecedent events and/or consequences associated with the behavior. Over time, the behavior will be molded and will of necessity be changed with the consistent application of the identified interventions.

38. D: Minority groups are a subset of individuals with differing characteristics. Feelings of marginalization, harassment, and/or oppression are insufficient criteria for minority status. By any such definition, virtually any individual might qualify as a minority. Rather, minority groups are identified in a primary social population as individuals possessing unique physical, social, and/or cultural characteristics. Due to their unique characteristics, minority group members tend to be oppressed, marginalized, and/or harassed by members of the primary population. Those who work with minority group members need to learn and be responsive to the unique burdens and needs of the group within which they are working.

39. B: According to the NASW Standards for Cultural Competence, the most important need for self-awareness in matters of diversity is to better appreciate the beliefs and cultural values of others. The first five of ten NASW Standards for Cultural Competence are:

1. Ethics and values – Recognizing how professional standards, values, and ethics might impact diverse clients.
2. Self-awareness – Recognizing how personal cultural beliefs and values can aid in understanding and responding to diversity in others.
3. Cross-cultural knowledge – The need for a deep understanding of diversity in the clients served.
4. Cross-cultural skills – The development of skills required to best serve diverse clients.
5. Service delivery – Identifying optimum resources and referrals for individuals with diverse backgrounds.

40. A: Standing up for oneself and one's rights are key components of assertiveness training, which are being demonstrated in this group. Positive thinking, healthy communication and stress reduction would be secondary skills utilized to foster assertiveness.

41. C: Cultural competence refers to the policies, behaviors, and attitudes to work well with people regardless of race, religion, class or culture. True cultural competence stems from the capacity to identify, accept, and affirm the intrinsic value of every person regardless of their differences, whether they are due to disabilities, age, gender, orientation, race, religion, culture, ethnicity, language, etc. Cultural proficiency formally refers to the degree of skill one possesses in managing these differences effectively. To work well in diverse settings, professionals must possess sufficient cultural proficiency to avoid compromising the mental or emotional wellbeing of those with diverse backgrounds.

42. B: Treat others as one desires to be treated is NOT an element of culturally competent practice. In point of fact, the way one wishes to be treated may, in itself, be specific to their culture, value system, and other beliefs. Thus, it becomes necessary to discover the specific way that others need to be treated to feel valued and supported, as opposed to assuming that one's needs and theirs will naturally be congruent and mutually acceptable. Effective organizations will recruit persons from diverse backgrounds, develop culturally sensitive policies and programs, and require cultural self-assessments and ongoing training of their staff.

43. D: The physician should follow the patient's wishes and inform the husband. The duty to inform a patient of the risks and benefits of a medical procedure does not translate into a duty to be informed. A patient possessing decisional capacity has the right to defer informed consent. The physician may wish to secure a waiver to that end, but it would be as unethical to coerce a patient into accepting information they clearly refused as it would be to deliberately withhold the information altogether.

44. A: The social worker should report the behavior to a designated child protective agency. There are limits to tolerance for cultural practices. Situations of child abuse must be reported in accordance with state law regardless of the cultural context. While it is good to seek assurance from the family that the practice will be stopped, it is insufficient to ensure the safety of the children involved. Child protective services staff are in a better situation to evaluate and monitor the process of behavior change, and to maintain an ongoing record to determine if any pattern of abuse has or will yet continue.

45. A: The formal definition of prejudice is to have negative thoughts or feelings about minority groups based solely on negative stereotypes, values, and judgments. Discrimination involves putting negative thoughts and feelings into action (actually impeding choices, options, benefits, etc., in response to feelings of prejudice). A bias may simply reflect a personal preference without negative overtones, and being judgmental typically refers primarily to an overall critical approach.

46. C: Religion is not a minority classification. The four most common minority group classifications are 1) race, 2) gender, 3) sexual orientation, and 4) age. The five most common racial/ethnic group classifications are: Asian, Black, Hispanic, Native American, and White. Stereotypes and over-generalizations based on race are typically referred to as racism. Those involving gender are referenced as sexism. When age is an untoward issue, it is referred to as ageism. Prejudices reflecting sexual orientation include homophobia (irrational feelings regarding gays and lesbians) and may extend to bisexual, and transgender people.

47. D: Ethnocentrism, the tendency to see one's own ethnicity and cultural patterns as superior and/or more acceptable, is largely universal. A sense of normative familiarity tends to reinforce comfort with such attributes, as well. Therefore, social workers who work with ethnic groups and other minorities must remain vigilant to the influences of ethnocentrism, and must actively endeavor to better recognize, understand, and incorporate the customs, culture, and practices of the groups with which their clients are associated.

48. B: Assessment is the first stage of treatment. It is crucial that trust, empathy, and rapport are established, and ethical obligations be explained, at the outset of a clinical relationship. Formal contracting must occur, covering mutual goals, roles, obligations, and the expected course of treatment. However, assessment is the first treatment step, and it should include:

- Personal history (significant health issues, marital status, etc.).
- Family (of origin and past/current family structure, roles, and relationships).
- Social (friends, hobbies, membership in organizations, etc.).
- Community (roles in civic affairs, politics, extended social circles, etc.).
- Religious and/or spiritual beliefs and practices.
- Emotional (coping skills, support systems, prior psychiatric history, and treatment).
- Intellectual (capacity, including education and training, etc.).
- Work (past and current employment history).
- Economic (financial status and recent changes, etc.).
- Legal (illicit substance abuse, arrests, incarcerations, etc.).

49. C: Changing one's perspective is a skill used in cognitive interventions, which teach clients new ways of thinking about problems and solutions. Notice that the other three options either assume the presence of another person (communication) or a mind-body approach, as in relaxation responses or environmental change.

50. A: Medical records are not a part of the social assessment. While some medical information may be relevant, to the degree it reflects aspects of a client's social functioning, other medical information would not be pertinent. The goal of a social assessment report is to determine the social and relationship issues that have bearing on a client's functional capacity and mental and emotional well-being. Of significant importance are the client's patterns of response to past crises and problems, as past behavior is the best predictor of future behavior.

51. D: Genograms (family-tree-like graphs) and ecomaps (family and social environment maps) are used to symbolically and graphically depict family and social relationships. They are particularly useful when the relationships are complex and extensive. Additional symbols, shapes, and lines assist in both defining the types of relationships and in identifying the impact the relationships have on the client in terms of overall support and functioning.

52. B: The social worker must arrange for hospitalization immediately. The client has been engaged in developing a specific plan for suicide, and other options—including contracting—should be deemed insufficient to ensure the client's safety. The lack of all materials necessary to carry out the suicide threat should not dissuade the social worker from taking this essential protective step, given the level of exploration and planning that the client has revealed. Other warning signs of suicide are a sudden escalation in alcohol or other substance abuse, reckless behavior, increased isolation and support system loss, feeling helpless and hopeless, other friends or family having attempted suicide, poor coping skills, and other unexplained changes in behavior.

53. A: The best response is to arrange for psychiatric hospitalization. The client will also need to be medically cleared, due to his poor health, and may end up being initially evaluated psychiatrically in the medical setting. The client has expressed significant suicidal ideation, has experienced a profound personal loss, is isolated (home bound), and refuses to sign a no-suicide contract. The contract is not in place unless it is signed. Thus, there is no formal agreement. Hospitalization should be pursued.

54. C: The social worker should evaluate the child for signs of physical abuse. The child is showing signs of hyper-vigilance and may well be experiencing physical abuse. Other signs include: unexplained injuries and bruises (especially when in varying stages of healing), attempts by a child to conceal injuries, excessive efforts by a child to please the parents, and major behavior problems (violence, running away, etc.). Children who are physically abused are also at risk for emotional and psychological abuse. Signs include: behavioral problems (acting out), appearing withdrawn, depression, rhythmic repetitive movements, untoward pressures to meet adult demands, and triangulation in marital conflicts. Signs of neglect include frequent school absences, inadequate attire, fatigue, poor hygiene, poor supervision, and being underweight or malnourished.

55. D: The social worker should suspect sexual abuse. Not all victims of sexual abuse will present as depressed or overwhelmed at their sexual experiences. Social workers should also be alert to children who are sexually aggressive, overly mature, promiscuous, physically inappropriate, and who present sudden gifts, money, toys, etc. Signs of more graphic abuse include physical injuries involving genitalia, signs of blood on the underclothing, bruises around the thighs and legs, enuresis or encopresis (incontinence of bladder or bowel after toilet training age, usually beyond age 4), phobias and fears, depression, suicidal thinking, self-destructive behavior, behavioral regression, dissociation, prostitution, and sexually transmitted diseases.

56. B: Wechsler Adult Intelligence Scale (WAIS) is the most commonly used IQ test in the US. Since the 1960's the Wechsler Intelligence Scales have been the most commonly used IQ tests in the United States. The Wechsler Preschool and Primary Scale of Intelligence-Revised (WPPSI-R) is used with children between the ages of 3 and 7. The Wechsler Intelligence Scale for Children (WISC) is used with children between the ages of 7 and 17, and the Wechsler Adult Intelligence Scale (WAIS) is used for adults. The Stanford-Binet Intelligence Scale is probably the next most frequently used scale for the measurement of intelligence in children. It was originally developed to help place children in appropriate educational settings.

57. D: International Classification of Diseases (ICD) was the precursor to the DSM. The International Classification of Diseases, first published in 1948 and now in its 10th edition, is used to classify diseases and other health problems recorded on many types of health and vital records and for epidemiological and quality evaluation purposes. It includes classification criteria for mental illnesses, along with all other health conditions currently identified. In 1952, the first Diagnostic and Statistical Manual of Mental Disorders (DSM) was published, and is now in its 6th edition, DSM-5. While the ICD remains in current use, most mental health clinicians use the DSM-5.

58. B: The likely diagnosis is avoidant personality disorder. The client is describing the features of avoidant personality disorder. Criteria include being worried about social situations, unwillingness to try new activities, avoiding activities once found enjoyable if they are social.

59. D: There is no Cluster D – only A, B, and C. These cluster descriptions have been provided by authors of various academic sources, although they only loosely describe each cluster's content. Cluster A includes: paranoid, schizoid, and schizotypal personality disorders. Cluster B includes: antisocial, borderline, histrionic, and narcissistic personality disorders. Finally, Cluster C includes: obsessive/compulsive, avoidant, and dependent personality disorders. Clusters tend to run in families.

60. C: V Codes are problems or conditions not due to a mental disorder, but that require clinical attention (e.g., noncompliance with treatment or parent-child relational problem). Most of these codes, borrowed from the International Classification of Disease (ICD) manual provide for severity and treatment course specifiers such as mild, moderate, and severe, as well as by prior history, in partial remission, or full remission. Where a specific diagnosis is expected, but has not been finalized, a code may be qualified as a provisional diagnosis. A diagnosis should also be accompanied by a diagnostic differential or formulation, in which the criteria in support of the diagnosis (and against other options) are summarized.

61. B: The client's right of self-determination must control the treatment process (except in situations of specific court-ordered treatment). While the social worker may suggest priorities, the broad goals and specific objectives of the treatment plan must be decided by the client, even if the social worker does not entirely agree. During the course of treatment, revisions to the focus and/or process of treatment (i.e., the treatment plan's goals and objectives) may become necessary and proper, but any such changes must ultimately be decided by the client and not imposed by the social worker.

62. D: The best initial response is to explore and discuss the client's feelings about termination. It may be possible to ameliorate the client's distress by exploring the feelings related to termination. This may well involve assuring the client that he or she can always return for further contact at any time, or even schedule a follow-up appointment in the near future. Revising the termination plan should not occur unless other reasonable options have been explored and attempted. Where early discussion about termination is incorporated in the initial treatment plan, and where accomplishment of client goals is tracked, noted, and discussed, healthy accommodation to termination is enhanced.

63. C: Early remission is no stimulant use criteria being met (except for craving) for at least 3 but less than 12 months. Sustained remission is no stimulant use criteria being met (except for cravings) for 12 months or longer. The terms full and partial are no longer used to describe remission.

64. B: The most likely diagnosis is mild neurocognitive disorder due to traumatic brain injury. A diagnosis of intellectual disability requires both cognitive impairment (an IQ of 70 or lower) and an onset before the age of 18. The condition would be identified as a neurocognitive disorder due to traumatic brain injury, given the history. Dementia is no longer used as a DSM-5 diagnosis- it has been subsumed under neurocognitive disorder.

65. A: The most appropriate diagnosis is oppositional defiant disorder. The degree of discord is substantial, and the level of verbal conflict is high, thus oppositional defiant disorder would be the most appropriate diagnosis. A parent-child relational problem (V61.20) tends to be less severe in nature, while conduct disorder is much more severe (i.e., involves violations of the rights of others, physical aggression, or property damage, persistent truancy, etc.). Intermittent explosive disorder addresses impulsive acts of aggression or violence (as opposed to premeditated or planned behaviors). Persistent conduct disorder carried into adulthood may meet criteria for antisocial personality disorder.

66. C: The most likely diagnosis is delirium. The key feature to delirium is a rapid onset and fluctuating course throughout the day. Dementia has been encompassed by the term neurocognitive disorder, which is characterized by a slow and persistent escalation of symptoms over an extended period of time. Diagnostically, the term senile is only an indicator of age (pre-senile refers to an onset prior to age 65; senile refers to an onset at age 65 or older). While overmedication is a possibility, there was not information provided to suggest this diagnosis, and thus the most likely diagnosis would be delirium due to a rapid onset medical condition (fever, bladder infection, early pneumonia, etc.) in an elderly individual.

67. C: The most appropriate diagnosis is stimulant use disorder. The DSM-5 no longer separates substances abuse and dependence but now places all disorders under substance use disorder, substance intoxication, and substance withdrawal. Stimulant use disorder involves the need for escalating amounts of a substance to achieve intoxication, withdrawal symptoms, compulsive use in spite of a desire to stop, compromised social, occupational/educational, familial, and/or other important role compromise due to the use of an intoxicating substance, and includes severe physiological or compulsive use features. Severity is decided by the number of symptoms, and can be classified as mild, moderate, or severe.

68. A: The most likely diagnosis is schizophrenia. Typical symptoms include: grossly disorganized or catatonic behavior and/or speech, delusions and/or hallucinations, blunted affect (poor or inappropriate expressive responses to external stimuli), autism (intense self-preoccupation). Continuous signs of symptoms must be present (allowing for waxing and waning fluctuations) for six or more months. There are five types: 1) paranoid; 2) disorganized; 3) catatonic; 4) undifferentiated; and, 5) residual. Early mild symptoms are sometimes referred to as prodromal schizophrenia. Common medications for treatment: Clozaril (clozapine), Haldol (haloperidol), Loxitane (loxapine), Mellaril (thioridazine), Prolixin (fluphenazine), Risperdal (risperidone), Stelazine (trifluoperazine), Thorazine (chlorpromazine), and Zyprexa (olanzapine).

69. C: The most likely primary diagnosis is major depression with psychotic features. The precipitating event was his job loss, which led to depression. As the depression deepened, he started hearing voices. He used alcohol use to cope with his depression and auditory hallucinations. The alcohol use must be included in the diagnostic formulation, but it would not be his primary diagnosis. Of note, the diagnosis of major depression with psychotic features is missed about 25% of the time in an emergency treatment setting, with only the depression typically identified.

70. B: The most likely diagnosis is panic disorder. Criteria for generalized anxiety disorder specifies excessive worry about a number of events or activities as opposed to an isolated fear or concern. Further, it tends to persist for long periods rather than having an abrupt onset. Somatization disorder is characterized by complaints regarding several organ systems involving different body sites and functions, rather a single body organ. Post-traumatic stress disorder requires confronting an event or events that involve actual or threatened death or serious injury. The client was away at school, did not witness his father's death, and it didn't pose any direct threat to him. Panic attacks involve sudden onset, profound fear of death, and other symptoms such as those the client has described. Common treatment medications: Paxil, Klonopin, Tofranil, Celexa, Librium, Valium, Xanax.

71. A: Although lithium carbonate has been used for many years in the treatment of bipolar disorder, it is by no means the only medication used to treat the condition. In more recent years bipolar disorder has been treated with: 1) anticonvulsants (i.e., certain anti-seizure medications); 2) antidepressants, such as selective serotonin reuptake inhibitors (SSRIs), monoamine oxidase inhibitors (MAOIs), and, less commonly, tricyclic antidepressants; 3) antipsychotics, such as Haldol and Zyprexa; 4) calcium channel blockers (including blood pressure medications such as Nifedipine and Verapamil); and 5) Benzodiazepines, such as Xanax and Valium. Even electroconvulsive therapy has been successfully utilized.

72. C: The most appropriate diagnosis would be social phobia. The typical symptoms of panic disorder (dizziness, shortness of breath, palpitations, profuse sweating, tingling, hyperventilation, etc.) are absent. General anxiety disorder is focused more on excessive worry and stress about a variety of issues, and it persists in spite of any specific location or activity. Social phobia involves fears about being in social situations involving performance and scrutiny. While bodily function fears lend to a diagnosis involving agoraphobia, the site-specific nature of this situation validates the greater likelihood of a social phobia.

73. B: The most appropriate determination would be malingering (though it is a V code, other conditions that may be a focus of clinical attention, and it is not a diagnosis). Malingering involves feigning symptoms primarily to derive an <u>external reward</u> (lawsuit settlement, disability benefits, etc.). Illness anxiety disorder involves a misapprehension or misinterpretation of bodily symptoms. Factitious disorder involves a feigning of symptoms primarily in order to receive the attention offered when one assumes a sick role, even in the absence of external reward. Somatic symptom disorder is characterized by complaints regarding several organ systems involving different body sites and functions rather than a single body organ or situation.

74. C: The most likely diagnosis is borderline personality disorder. The key features of BPD involved instability in relationships and affect, poor self-image, and high impulsivity. Violations of personal rights and apathy common to antisocial personality disorder are insufficiently pronounced. While evidence of histrionic behavior exists, the devaluation/over-valuation pattern common to BPD is not accounted for via histrionic personality disorder. Nor is the need for admiration, pervasive with narcissism, not otherwise addressed.

75. C: Selection of a practice framework should not be based solely on the model most commonly used by other social workers. Various factors may constrain the practice framework chosen, but it should never be a matter of "popularity" alone. It may become necessary to utilize more than one framework, based upon a clientele's needs, the course of treatment, demands of an agency or an insurer. Regardless, when utilizing a practice framework, it should guide the social worker's approach with the client, and the treatment process.

76. D: Behavioral and cognitive approaches are practice approaches based on theoretical orientations, not frameworks. The ethnic-sensitive framework requires the social worker to view and engage issues from an ethnic and cultural perspective, and the feminist framework orients engagement from the perspective of gender and feminism. The systems framework focuses on behavioral issues as related to biological and social systems. The eco-system framework views behavior from an environmental adaptation perspective. The strengths framework focuses on issues from the vantage point of a client's strengths and the capacity to achieve goals. Finally, the generalist framework provides for an eclectic approach, utilizing a variety of frameworks and approaches as necessary.

77. C: The proper response would be confronting the issue of resistance and making a point of addressing and exploring it with the client. The psychoanalytic (or psychodynamic) approach provides for direct confrontational address in situations of resistance. Drawing from psychoanalytic theory, ego psychology theory, object relations theory, and psychosocial theory, this theoretical orientation sees resistance as a way to avoid bringing up repressed memories, and unconscious/subconscious information necessary to growth, understanding, and overcoming.

78. C: The cultural formulation interview guide assists social workers in coming to an understanding of how the client's culture impacts his or her experience and current feelings and functioning. Such an interview should help social workers increase their cultural awareness and identify a change incident of cultural bias, as well as letting clients know that their heritage matters and is not being ignored or denigrated.

79. B: According to the psychoanalytic approach, treatment is NOT, by design, a short-term process, not to exceed six to twelve months. The psychoanalytic approach is generally a long-term therapeutic orientation, as time is required to identify, expose, and resolve repressed and unconscious information, experiences, drives and motivations that produce distortions and dysfunctions.

80. A: The behavioral approach is to identify and evaluate the antecedents and consequences of the behavior. In this way the social worker and client will be able to revise the antecedents and consequences in such a way as to induce change. In setting goals and measuring progress, the behavior will be need to be operationally defined (i.e., a vague problem, such as aggression, must be made explicit and measurable--frequency of hitting, throwing things, yelling, etc.), thus allowing for the identification of targets for change, quantified goal setting, and setting positive and negative reinforcers. In general, unconscious motivations, drives, and emotions are not seen as relevant to the goal of behavioral change, from a modification standpoint.

81. B: The technique most likely to help improve the client's confidence would be sustainment. This technique involves reaching out, and supplying acceptance, encouragement, and reassurance to enhance the client's internal fortitude, sense self-worth, and ultimate confidence. Delving into the past is an explorative process, rather than in intervention in itself. Ventilation is allowing a client unfettered expression to relieve into pressures, fears, and concerns. Dream analysis seeks meaning in dreams, and is not likely to enhance personal confidence in and of itself.

82. D: The goal of this activity is to identify behavioral frequency, intensity, and patterns, NOT resistance. It is important for the social worker to identify when target behaviors occur, what the client does about the behavior, and the specific feelings elicited by engaging in the behavior. These associated elements will allow the social worker to more effectively design reinforcement techniques that will lead to the perpetuation of desirable behaviors and the extinguishment of behaviors that are undesirable.

83. C: This technique is known as paradoxical direction. It represents a cognitive approach to behavioral change. The cognitive approach sees behavior as emerging directly from thoughts and cognition, and thus it is best changed by identifying, confronting, and altering specific misconceptions and false beliefs. The approach focuses on the present, and is problem-focused and goal oriented. In the parenting situation described here, if the child screams and yells the parent remains in control as the child is behaving as instructed. If the child does not resort to tantrum behavior, the parent is still in control because the child has made a constructive, desirable choice. Over time, the child learns that tantrum behavior is futile and non-productive, and ceases it as a natural course of events.

84. B: This client is experiencing retroflection. A person experiencing retroflexive behavior treats himself as he actually wanted to treat other persons or objects. Introjection is to do as others want one to do. Projection occurs when a person acts toward others what he accuses them of acting to him. A person experiencing confluence does not know who is doing what to whom because the boundaries between self and others are too vague. Finally, a person experiencing the retroflection acts toward himself as he would like to act toward others. Prolonged and/or intense retroflection can lead to depression and even self-destructive behavior.

85. D: This intervention perspective is called the Gestalt approach. Using this approach, the social worker is more a facilitator than a traditional social worker. The goals of this intervention are three-fold: 1) to increase self-awareness of key behaviors; 2) to identify and develop alternate behaviors; and, 3) to own and take responsibility for all behavioral choices.

86. A: The principle that long-term treatment is necessary to induce change is NOT part of the task-centered approach. The task-centered approach is intended to be structured like a short-term intervention. The treatment process typically takes place during 6-12 sessions, with the total treatment interval not generally exceeding several months.

87. C: This client is in Kübler-Ross's third stage of grief: bargaining. Elizabeth Kübler-Ross described five stages of grief. The first stage is denial, and is a defense mechanism to escape the awful reality of a loss. The second stage is anger, typically focused on the unfairness and/or pain at the loss. The third stage is bargaining, and is characterized by "if only" and "what if" questions. The fourth stage is despair (or depression), and is characterized by feeling the overwhelming sadness of a loss. The fifth stage is acceptance and is characterized by an acknowledgement of reality and a belief in eventual recovery.

88. B: The most effective intervention in this situation would be the crisis intervention approach. Crisis intervention recognizes the need for immediate, effective intervention, and a five-stage crisis sequence: 1) acknowledgement of the catastrophic/overwhelming event; 2) a sense of profound vulnerability that overmasters the client's usual coping skills; 3) a last straw precipitating event causing the individual to seek help; 4) emotional turmoil and imbalance; and 5) the application of new and/or more effective coping skills leading to adequate adjustment and acceptance.

89. C: This approach is the narrative approach. This family therapy approach suggests that behavior change occurs when family members produce alternate narratives, stories, or scenarios with improved endings by which to focus their energies and beliefs in a more positive way. Complementary therapy refers to supplemental intervention(s) that a social worker may use in addition to individual therapy. Collaborative therapy refers to family therapy provided by two or more social workers pursuing the same cooperative goals. The social learning approach seeks to teach family members added skills (conflict resolution, negotiation, communication, etc.) to address and resolve family dysfunction.

90. C: Strategic family therapy focuses on family rules and behavioral patterns. This approach suggests that persistent behavioral dysfunction and faulty family rules are at the heart of most family problems. Intervention is supplied by the social worker actively choosing to engage the family in ways that will highlight problematic behavioral patterns. In this way the family becomes more aware of problematic patterns of interaction, after which the social worker can assist the family in choosing more functional behaviors and interactive patterns.

91. A: The parent would benefit from joining an educational group. There are 7 major group types. Educational groups are formed to provide education, information, and essential skills. This parent needs to learn ways to manage medications, changing blood sugar, dietary needs, signs and symptoms of medical compromise, and so forth. An educational group is an ideal setting to learn how to provide optimum care and cope with inevitable changes and problems. A support group focuses on coping with a common problem (i.e., bereavement, etc.), but with less of an emphasis on learning and skill development. A self-help group is focused on behavioral change (i.e., alcoholics anonymous, etc.). A task group focuses on accomplishing a singular goal. Other group forms include: remedial groups (or psychotherapy groups, focused on personal growth, such as anger management), growth groups (developing personal potential), and socialization groups (to enhance interpersonal skills).

92. B: This group structure is a natural group. The group occurred naturally, and pre-existed the presence of the social worker. Some concern exists in formal settings, such as a hospital, when natural groups form. A primary concern is when misinformation emerges and is perpetuated via the group. Therefore, it may become necessary for the group to be formalized. In this situation an open group structure (that allows members to join and leave as they desire) may be advantageous. A closed group typically has set meeting times and an end-date (10 weeks, etc.), fosters greater intimacy and group cohesion, and allows for graduated information and teaching. It will of necessity be a short-term structure, as pediatric patients will ultimately be discharged. Formed groups are intentionally arranged, such as a court-ordered group for drug offenders.

93. D: The best course of action is to disclose limited information. Personal revelations are normally discouraged in a therapeutic relationship. They can turn the counseling experience into a mutual sharing process, robbing the client of proper attention. They can also cause the client to devalue the social worker if any revelation comes as an unwanted surprise. An exception to this rule exists when the therapeutic context is entirely centered in the information to be revealed—such as in a drug and alcohol rehabilitation program, where the sole purpose of the counseling is to address the issue being revealed (usually a group setting, where self-disclosure is essential to the process). Disclosures must not occur early, before trust is in place, and the group leader should always clearly understand his or her full intent and goals before revealing any personal information.

94. D: Effective group leadership does not include recruiting membership to ensure a large and diverse population, ideally consisting of more than 20 group members. Most theorists indicate that effective groups should not have memberships exceeding 8-12. The younger the group membership, the smaller the ideal group (preteens: 3-4; teens: 6-8; young adults: 8-10).

95. B: The most effective way of organizing group work is by first specifying the group's objectives. All other tasks can only be successfully pursued once the group's goals and objectives have been clarified. The other options presented could actually be addressed and incorporated or dismissed during the goal and objective clarification process.

96. C: This is an indication that the group has entered Stage 4: Differentiation. During this stage, group members display opinions and differing views more readily. Stage 1, pre-affiliation, involves getting acquainted and group appraisal. Stage 2, power and control, involves the development of roles and leadership within the group. Stage 3, intimacy, refers to the development of group cohesion and solidarity. Stage 5, separation, involves preparation for termination, including goal review, anticipated loss, and closure.

97. C: The supervisor's approach is most likely based on the systems theory. This theoretical paradigm postulates that individuals, their environment, and their situations are closely interrelated. Change in any one area will therefore result in changes in other areas. Consequently, any effective intervention must account for the total life situation involved. Systems theory departs from traditional psychological views which tend to largely utilize cause-and-effect models of behavior, suggesting that either the environment or the individual is primarily responsible for any given effect or outcome.

98. B: These changes could be referred to as adaptation. Eco-systems theory (also known as life model theory) postulates that all individuals experience adaptation by which they attempt to achieve a "goodness of fit" to their physical and social environment. Thus, this blended family adapted by revising roles, rearranging the home as needed, and altering schedules and activities to accommodate each other.

99. D: The best family therapy approach for this scenario is the social learning approach. This approach postulates that communication problems lie at the root of most or all family problems. The narrative approach suggests that thoughts, pre-conceived ideas, and personal stories drive behaviors, and that revising these pre-conceptions, story endings, and distorted ideas will lead to behavioral change. The structural approach focuses on patterns of interaction and relationships in a family and the revision of roles and family scripts. The social learning approach utilizes principles from behavioral therapy to overcome problematic behavior patterns that underlie communication problems and conflicts.

100. A: A social worker utilizing a Gestalt approach would refer to this phenomenon as confluence. This term refers to a tendency to reject, ignore, or deny any real differences between situations or experiences in favor of focusing on exaggerated or outright false perceptions of similarities. Projection occurs when an individual inaccurately attributes their own negative qualities to another individual. Introjection involves the inaccurate and inappropriate receipt and internalization of messages from others. Retroflection involves acting toward one's self in the way one actually desires to act toward another.

101. D: Crisis intervention is oriented toward problem-solving and is short-term in nature, typically concluding as soon as the zenith of a crisis has passed. The social worker must have sufficient expertise in the crisis issue (grief, suicide, rape, etc.) to be effective—quickly producing a meaningful sense of confidence and security through which to properly moderate the overwhelming feelings being experienced by the client. Yet it is also essential that the social worker not foster dependency in the relationship with the client, who may be sufficiently overwhelmed as to be uncharacteristically needy.

102. B: The best response is to thoughtfully but explicitly address and explore the behavior. Ignoring the behavior offers the couple no opportunity to address and overcome it. Mentioning the behavior only casually allows it to be equally casually dismissed. Confronting a couple who is in pain from a profound loss and already in fragile state could be perceived as overly aggressive, potentially leading to diminished rapport and/or therapeutic estrangement.

103. B: Simply asking the client directly why he/she is unwilling to cooperate would be the least effective approach in overcoming the client's reluctance. The direct approach is sometimes ideal.

However, asking a why question can be particularly problematic in a situation of resistance because the client may feel judged or challenged his response. The question itself suggests some belligerence or non-cooperation on the part of the client, and it can produce a confrontational situation that could damage the working relationship. Often asking a client to "tell me more about that" serves the same purpose, without the potential for disrupting the relationship.

104. A: The social worker's best response would be to aid the client in exploring his difficulties in this area. It would be helpful to the client to explore his reluctance further, certainly in deference to his capacity to work well in other opposite-gender relationships. If the client remains entirely unwilling to address the issue, or if subsequent exploration does not resolve the client's concerns, then a case transfer or referral out would be most appropriate.

105. B: The first step should be to acknowledge the highly ambivalent feelings she is experiencing. There is a natural tendency is to hasten and point out the classic features of relationship abuse. However, this approach is likely to immediately alienate the client. Importantly, she has already expressed ambivalent feelings. Allowing her to process those feelings, and then moving on to exploring other past relationships, and eventually reality-testing this one is typically much more successful approach.

106. C: The most appropriate response is to use reflective listening techniques and allow the client more time. Aggressive and/or confrontational techniques are unlikely to induce change in a client with a predisposition to defer to others. It becomes necessary to more skillfully apply reflective listening techniques to bring this client out. This will require the social worker to be more tolerant of a slower therapeutic pace, and carefully guard against completing the client's sentences to overcome awkward pauses and periods of silence.

107. A: At this point the social worker should revise the meeting to cover only very basic issues until other arrangements can be made. Abruptly terminating a meeting may leave the client feeling rejected and upset after the efforts she has made to attend. Delaying the meeting can cause similar problems. Having her contact a friend or relative to assist will leave her unable to speak freely and privately about any problems or concerns she is having. Therefore, revising the meeting to pursue only basic information intake and to establish simple rapport would be advantageous.

108. C: "Okay" declarations are not examples of furthering responses. In some situations, the word okay may be taken as a conversation conclusion—perceived as meaning "I understand, and no further explanation or discussion is necessary." Thus, other furthering responses would more likely cause a client to continue sharing.

109. C: Optimum orientation would be to have the social worker and client angled toward one another, about 90 degrees. This orientation suggests collaboration and mutuality without the more confrontational feel that may arise in direct face-to-face seating. While a therapy couch may be used in some situations, it is no longer seen as an ideal orientation for most therapeutic encounters. Sitting with a desk in between can produce a power gradient that reduces the likelihood of open communication, and thus is to be discouraged.

110. C: SA question that contains multiple parts and may confuse or be unclear to a client, or make the client uncertain which part to answer first, is known as a stacked or complex question. "Was the part that you didn't understand where he told you to stop, or where he asked for your supervisor, or where he said that you could be held liable for that?" This question can easily leave a client confused and uncertain how to respond. Feelings such as this can make the client less willing to communicate. It often results in a client not answer all parts of the question offered. It is far better to ask simpler two-part questions, which are far less likely to confuse or overwhelm a client. Additional questions can be asked to seek further clarity if uncertain remains or other issues had not been adequately queried.

111. B: Paraphrasing is used to clarify what the client said, while summarizing is used to provide an overview of what the client said. Paraphrasing is a modestly revised restatement of a client's words. It is used to show respect and demonstrate that one was listening attentively. Paraphrasing further emphasizes the client's message (e.g. "I felt rejected" to "I can see how you felt so abandoned"), and to confirm mutual understanding. Summarizing is providing an overview of the entire situation discussed to provide greater clarity and ensure mutual understanding.

112. B: Substitution ("What I would do is...") is not an element of reflective or active listening. For the social worker to choose to tell a client what he/she would do is problematic in many ways. First, it turns the conversation away from him or her and puts the focus on the social worker. Second, it derails his or her own thinking, as the client may feel he or she need do little more than be told what to do. Further, it closes off further discussion and exploration as the authority figure appears to have given a final word and that will likely leave the client feeling that the issues have been concluded.

113. D: This communication technique is called partialization. This involves taking complex ideas, thoughts, or concerns voiced by a client, and reducing them to smaller parts that the client can process and respond to more easily. Leading the client to understand what is occurring is important, to limit any sense of confusion. This may require a brief introduction. For example, "Well, if we take these things one at a time, maybe we can tackle this a little more easily."

114. B: "Could you tell me more about... [a situation] ...?" is an example of an open-ended, non-leading question. It explicitly encourages the client to continue and to share more. It offers no direct "opinion," and it does not suggest that the social worker is the preferred or only source for information on the topic being discussed. Further, it encourages the client toward additional self-exploration, which can to greater mutual understanding and added insights.

115. A: Regardless of the method of communication, the recipient of information must process or interpret then information by means of decoding. Communication is a two-part process, involving both the sending and receiving of information. This remains true, regardless of the method of communication involved (i.e., verbal, written, symbolic, body language, etc.). The recipient of any communication is required to decode the information in order to perceive, understand, and respond to the information that was received.

116. B: The most likely result, according to the social exchange theory, would be premature therapeutic termination by the client. Social exchange theory (Thibault and Kelley, 1952) addresses perceptions about fairness, balance, and costs versus benefits in relationships. Relationships are characterized as an exchange process. Individuals seek to minimize costs and maximize rewards, and anticipate that their acts will be noticed and reciprocated in some way. Where a steep relational imbalance occurs (i.e., high-level confrontation), relationships are compromised and termination becomes likely unless the party feels no other options exist.

117. D: Social learning theory (Bandura, 1973, 1977) postulates that observation, imitation, and modeling are primary routes of learning. Therefore, when a social worker demonstrates enhanced communication skills by way of role play or dialogue modeling, social learning theory is being applied. The environment also reinforces or punishes modeling (i.e., by means of acceptance or rejection), leading to accelerated acceptance or extinguishment of the interaction patterns selected.

The theory has often been called a bridge between behaviorist and cognitive learning theories, although an increased cognitive emphasis has been noted in recent years.

118. B: The social role theory most likely explains his distress. Social role theory (Parsons, 1951) posits that one's behaviors, predispositions, and desires arise through a set of specific socially determined roles internalized during the socialization process of the formative years. Gender roles, such home-maker or breadwinner, are among the stronger role expectations. Where expected roles are not validated (i.e., a man should work outside the home as a provider – usually interpreted as earning more financially), relational distress can arise.

119. C: According to Drisko (2009), the fifth of five key factors required for a quality therapeutic relationship between client and clinician is the use varying types of empathy.

120. A: These are all stages of group development. During these stages, the social worker needs to: 1) facilitate familiarity and elicit participation; 2) clarify roles; 3) develop group cohesion; 4) support individual differences; and 5) foster independence. The use of a sociogram (a chart or diagram depicting group member relationships) can aid the social worker in revealing, monitoring, and intervening (if necessary) in group member interactions and bonding.

121. D: The social worker is acting in the role of case manager. A social work case manager actually arranges for the provision of services for a client, based upon a proper needs assessment and evaluation. Then the social work case manager monitors the services provided, and secures alternate resources and services as dictated by changes in the client's status. By contrast, a social worker acts as a broker when the client is provided linkage information for various services and resources, but the client actually applies for, secures, and monitors the appropriateness of those resources personally. A social worker serves an educational role when teaching, and an advocate role when defending, representing, and supporting a client's needs for services, programs, or policy accommodation.

122. C: The most difficult issue when treating reluctant or involuntary clients is client ambivalence about the need for treatment. Clients who are receiving involuntary treatment are often angry at being forced into the clinical setting. However, from a clinical perspective, client ambivalence about whether or not there is a need for treatment is often the greatest obstacle to be overcome. It is not possible to make meaningful improvement if a client does not see any need to change.

123. D: The underlying story of this client is that the client is conflicted about leaving her husband. The client doesn't consciously connect that conflict with her car-related phobia, but the social worker notes that anxiety and panic attacks do not happen with other people. In this case, the latent content of the client's story may be that driving is a metaphor for her life.

124. B: The steps upon first meeting a client should be establishing a rapport usually includes a review of the client's presenting problem, fostering trust, showing empathy and concern, and demonstrating a willingness to be non-judgmental about the presenting issue. Summarizing legal and ethical obligations includes addressing mandatory reporting issues and client confidentiality. A service contract covers mutual roles and expectations, major goals, the anticipated course of treatment, and how to handle issues of non-performance. Assessment includes the client's mental health history, medical history (including substance abuse), family history, work history, and social history. It may also include an evaluation of the client's mood, safety, intellectual functioning, and emotional stability.

125. D: These approaches are associated with family therapy. This modality also uses the strategic family therapy approach, which focuses on the function of family rules and behavior patterns. The goal of the social worker is to devise interventions, which will elicit functional behavioral patterns, and revise those family rules, which defeat or impede appropriate family relationships and conduct.

126. C: The best way to resolve this issue is to seek supervisory or other consultation to explore the situation further. In an agency setting, a supervisor is available. In private practice, and clinical consultant is typically available. Exploration with a supervisor or consultant may resolve the issue, or transfer (within an agency) or referral (outside the agency or practice) may become necessary. Client well-being and proper therapeutic boundaries are paramount.

127. B: In this situation the social worker is serving primarily in the role of broker. This role involves linking clients to various resources and services for which they may qualify. An advocate, on the other hand, represents, defends, or otherwise acts in behalf of one or more clients as related to needed policies, programs, or other actions.

128. B: The primary client is the wife. Initially, the identified client would be the husband. Upon entry of the wife into the picture, the identified client would be the couple, given that the social worker as working with them both and seeing them only jointly. After the passage of time, however, and upon identification of issues requiring primary work with the wife, the identified client would be the wife. Ideally, the social worker would have come to some measure of closure with the husband, identifying specifically that the focus had shifted from them as a couple to a primary endeavor with the wife. Regardless, the information now being entered in the clinical record is exclusively that related to the wife, and the husband should no longer be privy to that content. In keeping with this, the identified client has become the wife.

129. B: Building the profession to be superior to other social and psychological interventionists is NOT a part of the NASW's mission of social work. The social work profession is collaborative, and recognizes other professions, practitioners, and interventionists as having singular and important contributions to be made in meeting individual and societal needs.

130. C: Although socio-environmental factors are deemed to be important in the practice of social work, acclimation and accommodation are not "core values" of social work. Core values address the overall endeavor of the profession, not just ancillary segments or singular elements of the therapeutic process.

131. A: This is known as informed consent. Generally, the scope of informed consent extends to information that a rational person would want to know before making a decision for or against a proposed therapeutic option. The social worker is also responsible for ensuring the requisite information is presented in a way that the client can understand in order to determine that a fully informed consent has been obtained. For instance, when a client is mentally ill, underage, or showing signs of senile dementia, consent should be obtained via a legal guardian or through the courts.

132. C: In situations of suspected child abuse, the social worker can freely breech client confidentiality without informed consent. Every state in the U.S. has child abuse reporting laws, and allows reports to be made without regard to confidentiality and even in situations where the abuse is merely suspected in good faith. However, law enforcement officials are no automatically entitled to confidential client information, and even a court subpoena does not necessarily grant a social worker the right to freely disclose confidential information. Consultation with an attorney familiar with the laws of the specific state involved would be ideal in situations of subpoena.

133. B: In this case, where Jim advises her mother on finances, which may affect her as well, it's a reasonable, sensible, and ethical decision to refer Jim to another social worker. Terminating the relationship without a referral is not for the best interest of the client.

134. B: Regardless of the compelling nature of the information, or the good it might do others, records cannot be released for publication without consent from the individual. While PL 93-579 applies only to federal agencies and settings, virtually all state and local government agencies have promulgated these same practices.

135. D: Employer and supervisor liability accrue under the legal theory of vicarious liability. Although an agency may have liability insurance, it is usually recommended that individual social workers carry their own private coverage. Agency responsibility typically ends at the margins of the scope of the social worker's employment duties (unless agency staff knew in advance of an employee's misconduct and took no protective action). Agency liability continues even off the premises, to the degree the employee's scope of duties extends off the premises.

136. B: The initial response should be to explore both treatment and non-treatment views and options. All parties involved should be provided with all information and views for fully informed consent. Ethically, although he has not attained the age of majority, his views should be given considerable weight and, depending upon his maturity, may prove controlling should the matter end up in court. Advocating against the parents' choice can be problematic, as can advocating against the teenager. To avoid this, it is important to take the time to explore the relevant views of both the parents and the teen. As the outcome of the condition is known in advance (terminal), any treatment goals need to be meaningful and clear.

137. C: The proper response is to call the girlfriend and let her know that they have concerns given his level of agitation when he left the office. Tarasoff regulations specify a duty to warn if: 1) a serious threat of physical violence is made; 2) the threat is made against a specifically named individual(s); and, 3) the threat is also made in the context of a clinician-patient relationship. The duty to warn stems from the 1976 legal case Tarasoff v. Regents of the University of California where a social worker heard a credible threat and only called law enforcement authorities (failing to notify the intended victim). However, in this case, the client's extensive history, immediate behavior, and veiled verbiage appears to arise to a threshold of a duty to warn.

138. A: The most appropriate response is to tell the client that if she does not discontinue the behaviors or have the boyfriend inform the social worker that he is aware, the social worker will be required to warn him over her objections. A situation where a client is HIV positive and is known to be having unprotected sex or needle-sharing with a victim who is not aware of the client's HIV positive status falls under the Tarasoff duty to protect. Given the deadly nature of the sexually and blood-to-blood transmitted HIV, it has been determined that a social worker or other clinician may be warranted in breaching confidentiality if it can be demonstrated that counseling about transmission dangers have failed to alter an HIV positive client's behavior. However, the following five specific criteria must be met:

- The client must be known to be HIV positive.
- The client must be engaging in unprotected sex or sharing drug injection paraphernalia.
- The behavior must actually be unsafe.
- The client must indicate intent to continue the behavior even after counseling regarding potential harm.
- HIV transmission must be likely to occur.

139. B: The incidence of both mild and major traumatic brain injury (TBI) has risen profoundly in recent conflicts. Also, sexual assault trauma is often overlooked, particularly if the veteran is male. While combat stress (battle fatigue) is the primary trigger for posttraumatic stress disorder (PTSD), both of these other traumas can also contribute substantially to PTSD as well as other difficulties encountered in re-entering the civilian world. Military sexual trauma (MST) rates run 22% among female veterans and 1.2% among males. Mild traumatic brain Injury (mTBI) is overlooked particularly often, as it does not require loss of consciousness or even a diagnosable concussion to later become an issue. Any substantial blow to the head, or even close proximity to certain kinds of explosive blasts, can induce it—either immediately or in a delayed form. Key symptoms are unexplained episodes of confusion, disorientation, loss of concentration, feeling dazed, etc. In such situations, neuropsychiatric consultation is essential.

140. A: The Health Insurance Portability and Accountability Act of 1996 (HIPAA) applies to all health care providers, health care clearinghouses, and health plan providers. It sets limits on the disclosure and use of patient records. It also provides for individual access to medical records and establishes the right to receive notices of privacy practices.

141. B: There is no requirement that information be disclosed to an employer providing coverage, unless the employee has previously stipulated information to be released in consent for coverage and services. Payment for coverage by an employer does not, in and of itself, entitle the employer to any private client information. Even under conditions of subpoena, social workers may be able to limit the scope of information shared, or even claim "privileged communication" status in response to orders to testify.

142. D: Before a social worker can release any information from discussions with a client or from a client's case records, several requirements must be met. The client must agree and sign that information can be released. Further, informed consent for information must have been provided. Specifically, the client must understand the purpose for which the information is being released, where/to whom the information is being released, and from what period of time and during what period of time the information is being made available. It is the obligation of the releasing part to ensure the client is informed and fully understands why information is being released.

143. C: The brother has a moral obligation but no legal liability. Agency, staff, secretaries and/or clerical support, and formal volunteers are legally liable to maintain confidentiality. However, the brother of the secretary is not a formal volunteer. He was not provided any formal orientation, he did not sign a confidentiality agreement, nor was his role supposed to expose him to privileged information. While there is always a moral obligation to maintain an individual's privacy and confidential information, it does not extend to a legal obligation. Ethics, in this context, refers to the obligations of a particular class of professionals, not incidental lay persons. In this case, the professionals violated their ethical and professional standards, and do have legal accountability for this breech.

144. C: Records may be withheld based upon issues of a possible adverse reaction. In situations where a client is likely to have an adverse reaction (i.e., severe psychological compromise, issues of safety regarding the client and/or others), records may be withheld. A summary may be provided to the client, containing relevant information, but the agency may refuse to release copies based upon safety and/or adverse reaction grounds.

145. D: Services "in the trenches," such as frontline organizational services, are provided by employee staff, not administrators. Planning, delegation, conflict resolution, mediation, and advocacy are all basic functions of administrators.

98

146. C: Interdepartmental funding allocation is something done at the administrative level, rather than by supervisory staff. A supervisor's role includes being a role model, recruitment and orientation, day-to-day management, staff training, staff education, staff development, staff assessments and staff reviews.

147. C: Consultants may be empowered to act very broadly or very narrowly, depending upon their assignment(s). Supervisors, however, invariably have an assignment of discrete scope and authority.

148. C: This approach is referred to as the personality perspective. The interactional perspective refers to the processes of interaction between the supervisee and the supervisor. The situational perspective focuses on issues and issue resolution. The organizational perspective addresses policy, procedure, and organizational goals and objectives. Supervisors typically use a combination of these perspectives in overseeing and guiding staff.

149. C: Supervisors should provide staff meetings and/or individual staff supervision weekly. These encounters should be structured, consistent, oriented to case and/or situational reviews, and should result in evaluative feedback to the staff person(s) involved.

150. B: The most effective educational approach to employ in this situation is role playing. If the individual with whom the staff member engages in role play is properly skilled and educated, then this approach is superior to all others. The goal of supervision and training is to ensure that agency clients receive appropriate services, rather than ensuring that staff is well-trained, per se.

151. C: The best role of a supervisor in this situation is to urge the staff member to obtain professional counseling elsewhere. It is not appropriate for a supervisor to enter into a dual relationship with a staff member. The staff member should be encouraged to seek outside professional counseling assistance, and the supervisor should address only those issues that affect the staff person's ability to perform the work required.

152. C: The difference between statistical reliability and validity is that reliability requires consistent results over multiple test administrations, while validity refers to whether or not the test actually measures what it claims to measure.

153. A: This overall sampling approach is known as stratified random sampling, as the groupings occur via an identified common denominator (age), and simple random sampling followed for each stratum. Simple random sampling requires that participant selection based on a process where every client has an equal chance of being selected (i.e., via a random number generator, etc.). Systematic sampling involves selecting participants via a system (i.e., every fifth client in the appointment book). Cluster Sampling involves grouping participants into natural clusters and then sampling all within the cluster.

154. D: It would not be proper to tell medical staff that no help is available. Every effort should be made to assist. EMTALA regulations (Emergency Medical Treatment and Active Labor Act) require all patients who present at an emergency room to be stabilized before discharge in life-threatening health situations. This case might warrant further review. In 1975, Congress passed Title XVI as an amendment to the 1946 Hill-Burton Program. It established Federal grants, loan guarantees, and interest subsidies for health facilities and required them to provide certain levels of uncompensated services in perpetuity. This patient may qualify. Other sources of assistance may also exist. In short, efforts to assist should always be made.

155. B: Deinstitutionalization refers to changes in policy and law that led to the release of many disabled patients who would have otherwise remained in institutional settings. Involuntary hospital commitment (i.e., in an asylum) became increasingly common up to the 1950s, as had institutionalization of those otherwise disabled. However, the Community Mental Health Act of 1963 began to reverse this trend, as did the 1999 US Supreme Court ruling in Olmstead vs. LC. Laws mandating the least restrictive environment (LRE) for education and housing were also passed (i.e., see PL 94-1421, which requires education in the LRE). This era came to be called the era of deinstitutionalization. Sometimes overdone, issues of homelessness among the mentally ill and re-institutionalization in the prison system have been noted.

156. D: The social worker should first ensure that application is first made for worker's compensation. Because the injury occurred during the course and scope of the patient's employment, the first application made should be for worker's compensation. While he may eventually become eligible for social security disability (depending upon rehabilitation outcomes), supplemental security income (depending upon residual income), and/or Medicaid (if, for any reason he was found ineligible for worker's compensation (i.e., contributing issues such as drinking or drug use on the job, etc.), the patient's most likely and primary recourse will be worker's compensation.

157. C: To be eligible for full benefits, an individual born before 1960 must have the age of 65. The fully eligible retirement age incrementally increases to the age of 67 for individuals born in or after 1960, in order to qualify for full benefits. Those who retire before they achieve their fully vested retirement age may still qualify for benefits, but at a reduced rate. Social Security was never intended to be an individual's sole source of income. Individuals earn up to four tax credits per year, and must have a lifetime total of forty tax credits to receive benefits upon retiring.

158. D: The two specific components of Medicare were originally medical insurance and hospital insurance. Hospital insurance (Part A) covers necessary hospital, skilled nursing facility, home health, and hospice care. Medical insurance (Part B) covers doctors' services, preventive care, durable medical equipment, hospital outpatient services, laboratory tests, x-rays, mental health care, and some home health and ambulance services. Part C is not a separate benefit. It allows private insurers (such as such as HMOs and PPOs—sometimes known as Medicare Advantage plans) to provide Medicare benefits. Part D (Prescription Drug Insurance) provides outpatient prescription drug coverage. It is optional, and is provided only through private insurance companies that have contracts with the government.

159. D: These programs are funded federally and state administered. The Elderly Nutrition Program provides seniors (age 60 and over) food at churches and community centers. The Food Stamps program provides food purchase coupons to indigent families based on size and income. The School Lunch Program provides nutritional commodities to states for enhanced nutritional lunches, and free lunches for eligible poor children. The Women, Infants and Children (WIC) program offers food assistance to pregnant women, children under the age of five, mothers of children up to five months of age, and breastfeeding mothers with infants up to 12 months of age.

160. A: Demographic programs are not a category of government sponsored social service policies. Exceptional eligibility programs serve groups with special common needs (e.g., The Veterans Administration). Selective eligibility programs require certain eligibility criteria, and are means-tested (i.e., income or resource linked). Universal programs are available without any restriction or eligibility criteria.

161. B: Federal guidelines mandate that the health care provider must accept Medicaid as payment in full. Under Federal Title XIX of the Social Security Act, health care providers may not bill Medicaid patients for any service costs. The states may impose certain nominal deductibles, coinsurance, or co-payments for various services and for certain eligible groups. Even then, cost sharing is not permitted for pregnant women, children under age 18, hospital or nursing home patients, and indigent HMOs enrollees. Emergency services and family planning services are exempt from any co-payments for every Medicaid recipient.

162. B: Prior to 1996, the TANF program was known as Aid for Families with Dependent Children (AFDC). The legislated changed in 1996 was to transform AFDC into a temporary program designed to move recipients into the workforce.

163. C: The key deficiency inherent in a bureaucratic structure is the universal application of rigid rules and procedures. The bureaucratic approach works well for average cases and situations. However, when unique variables or circumstances arise, the rules and regulations of a bureaucratic organization may well become barriers to appropriate services and optimal resource allocation.

164. D: Providing front-line services to agency clients is NOT a basic administrative function. Primary staff provides front-line day-to-day services. Administrators are responsible for ensuring the effective functioning and outcomes of the services provided. Refining and reorganizing the agencies resources and objectives to maximize client services and outcomes is a key administrative role.

165. C: A key feature of non-profit organizations as compared to for-profit organizations is greater control over assets and revenue. Non-profit organizations have far less control over assets, resources, and revenue. Should a non-profit business be sold or liquidated, for example, the assets must be given to another non-profit for benefit of the community at large, and cannot be received by any owner, participant, or staff member, of the business.

166. A: Operating revenue refers to the funds derived through the provision of services and/ or goods. Operating support refers to funds derived from other sources besides the sale of goods and services (i.e., donations, grants, etc.). Expenses are the costs incurred for organizational operations. A surplus results when revenue and support exceeds operating expenses, whereas a deficit occurs when profits falls short of needed operating expenses. Gains or losses are reported from non-business operating transactions (i.e., the sale of business equipment, furniture, etc.). Net assets (after accounting for all revenue and expenses) are often referred to as the business' bottom line.

167. C: SOAP is a method of problem-oriented recording. SOAP refers to subjective (what an individual reports or says); objective (what is observed or revealed by testing); assessment (an interpretation of both subjective and objective findings); and, plan (formulation of a response to achieve a necessary outcome). Derived from a medical recording technique, it generally encompasses the four key elements of a problem-oriented record – 1) a data (factual information such as found on a factsheet); 2) a rank-order list of problems; 3) a plan (resolution steps); and, 4) progress notes regarding follow-up actions taken.

168. B: The most rigorous form of program outcome evaluation is an experimental evaluation. This approach uses experimental and quasi-experimental processes, including the effects of independent variables on an identified dependent variable, to test for causality as related to program efficacy. The decision-oriented approach involves an evaluation of existing agency data, along with observation, interviews, and surveys. The customer and peer review is typically limited to interviews and surveys only. A performance audit involves a third-party evaluator to reviews and rates program performance standards. Only the experimental evaluation approach actually tests program performance in a scientifically rigorous way.

169. D: The most effective approach to take would be a cluster evaluation. Cluster evaluations are optimum where multiple sites, programs, and interests are involved. The evaluative steps involve visiting each site, collecting records, orienting to each site, and identifying unique service plans, et cetera. Next a networking conference is held to identify commonalties and uniqueness among the programs. Cluster-level questions focus on information from early data collection and initial program analyses. Later conferences focus on findings and outcomes, with recommendations for change. Cluster evaluation involves many participants, and thus offers considerable certainty about the conclusions reached. Its primary limitations include the potential for bias and group-think to occur.

170. A: Ideally, both administrators and supervisors will share a common primary goal of quality client service. Administrators, however, pursue this goal through agency organization, programs, policies, funding, and other broad concerns. By contrast, supervisors pursue this goal through staff supervision, training, monitoring, performance reviews, continuing education, and competent hiring practices.

Thank You

We at Mometrix would like to extend our heartfelt thanks to you, our friend and patron, for allowing us to play a part in your journey. It is a privilege to serve people from all walks of life who are unified in their commitment to building the best future they can for themselves.

The preparation you devote to these important testing milestones may be the most valuable educational opportunity you have for making a real difference in your life. We encourage you to put your heart into it—that feeling of succeeding, overcoming, and yes, conquering will be well worth the hours you've invested.

We want to hear your story, your struggles and your successes, and if you see any opportunities for us to improve our materials so we can help others even more effectively in the future, please share that with us as well. **The team at Mometrix would be absolutely thrilled to hear from you!** So please, send us an email (support@mometrix.com) and let's stay in touch.

If you feel as though you need additional help, please check out the other resources we offer:

Study Guide: http://MometrixStudyGuides.com/ASWB

Flashcards: http://MometrixFlashcards.com/ASWB